The Path:

A 90-Day Journey to Living
God's Will
in Today's World

Suzanne Murray

Dedication & Acknowledgments

This book is dedicated, first and foremost, to the One who inspired every word of it—my Heavenly Father. Thank You for giving me life. Thank You for teaching me every single day of my life. Thank You for using me. I love You, LORD. I also dedicate this book to my wonderfully supportive husband, David, as well as my *own* two youth, David Jr. and Elizabeth. The desire to teach you well led me to the True and Wise Teacher, and I am the one who was taught. I love you, dear family.

I would like to offer many thanks to my editor, Paige Duke. In addition, I offer a special thanks to Linda Kennedy for all of her helpful advice.

Introduction

My loving parents knew the importance of raising my sister and me up in the care and nurture of the church. I am eternally grateful. From as far back as I can remember, we attended church. This included Sunday school, vacation Bible school, Christian preschool and kindergarten. I remember very clearly the day I prayed the prayer of salvation in my backyard. I've always loved God and have been assured of His forgiveness and my eternal life. What I didn't know was that there was so much more. How could it be that I could grow up in the church, be assured of my salvation, yet feel no differently, act no differently, and have nothing to show that I loved Jesus? I thank God for awakening in me a true hunger and thirst to know Him more. This hunger and thirst led me to His Word. From there, I discovered what I never even knew I'd been missing: the desire to walk *the path* of my life with my Loving, Heavenly Father.

Though I am a nurse by training, I've been teaching in the church for the past eighteen years, mostly as a volunteer. God has taught me so much during that time. I would never have dreamed that a shy, insecure, young mom could be used by a powerful, awesome, omniscient God! Thankfully, He tells us in His Word, "But this precious treasure—this light and power that now shine within us—is held in perishable containers, that is, in our weak bodies. So everyone can see that our glorious power is from God and is not our own" (2 Corinthians 4:7, NLT).

Over those eighteen years, God awakened in me a true passion for youth. I felt so inspired to share with them what God had taught me when I began to truly follow Him. I was blessed to serve as the youth director at my church for five years. During those five years, I spent so much time listening for and learning from God. He alone inspired the messages I shared with the youth. Now, my overwhelming desire is to share with each of you all that God has taught me. He has now called me to "Write down the revelation and make it plain on tablets so that a herald may run with it" (Habakkuk 2:2).

My desire is that the words God inspires in me will awaken in you a true hunger and thirst for Him. There *is* more, and He wants us to not only know that in our minds, but discover its truth in our hearts, as well. I pray this book will lead you to this discovery. It is life changing. "The path of the righteous is like the first gleam of dawn, shining ever brighter till the full light of day" (Proverbs 4:18).

Before I begin, do you know Jesus? This book is about discovery, and Jesus is woven into every part of that discovery. We *must* know Him. We must know and believe that Jesus is the Son of God (Mark 1:1). We must know and believe that Jesus became flesh and came to Earth to live with us (John 1:14). We must know and believe that Jesus fully obeyed God, never sinned, and became our sin for us (2 Corinthians 5:21). We must know and admit that we are sinners (Romans 3:23) in need of a Savior. We must know and believe that Jesus *is* that Savior, who died to take our place (Romans 6:23). And we must know and believe that Jesus is alive again (Matthew 28:5-6). Do you know and believe these things about Jesus? Have you declared your belief to God?

"That if you confess with your mouth, 'Jesus is Lord,' and believe in your heart that God raised him from the dead, you will be saved" (Romans 10:9).

This belief *is* the introduction to walking the path of your life with God. Jesus said that He is the only way to the Father (John 14:6).

I have written this guide to be read in a sequential fashion. Day One is for the very first day you start this book, no matter the date. The Bible verses listed at the end of each day are vital to understanding the text, and they highlight the Source that inspired me: God's Holy Word. Please take the time to look them up. If you don't have the version listed, you may find it online. On many days, you will find that the day's reading ends with a question. My hope is that you will meditate on these questions and let them inspire you to draw closer to God and apply His Words and each day's devotion in your own life. I pray that you will "grasp how wide and long and high and deep is the love of Christ, and to know this love that surpasses knowledge — that you may be filled to the measure of all the fullness of God," (Ephesians 3:18–20). May you be richly blessed as you read these words, inspired by our precious LORD. And may you *discover*.

Day One

Teach me your way, O LORD; lead me in a straight path because of my oppressors.

Psalm 27:11

Imagine that you're about to go on a long journey. You have the supplies you need, but as you start off, you realize there are two paths before you. One way looks like it would be easy on the feet, as it's paved with soft sand, but its surface is constantly changing and it looks a bit unpredictable. The other path may be less comfortable, as it is paved with rock, but its surface is solid and sure, and it looks more reliable. Which do you choose — more comfortable, yet unpredictable; or less comfortable, yet reliable?

In the same way, life is a journey. And, likewise, we have two paths before us. One path is paved with sand, and it represents the path walked apart from God. This path is unpredictable because it has us relying on ourselves, the people around us, and the world we live in for our security. And, as we know, we live in a world of constant change: Circumstances are always changing; people and events are always changing. Nothing stays the same.

The other path is paved with rock, and it represents the path walked with God. This path is reliable and sure because, as we are told in Malachi 3:6, "I the LORD do not change."

The events and circumstances and people in our life are going to change constantly, but God, our Father, will never change.

The direction that our life's journey takes is all about the path we choose. We're either walking with God or apart from Him. He leaves that choice up to us.

In what direction is your life's journey taking you?

Psalm 25:4 (NLT); Isaiah 26:7

Day Two

For no one can lay any foundation other than the one already laid, which is Jesus Christ.

1 Corinthians 3:11

Our life is a journey, and we get to choose the path we will walk on throughout that journey. Do we choose to walk alone, or do we choose to walk with God? God created us, God loves us, and He wants us to walk with Him, and follow His lead. In Deuteronomy 31:8 we are told, "The LORD himself goes before you and will be with you; he will never leave you nor forsake you. Do not be afraid; do not be discouraged." We are promised in His Word that He will never leave us nor forsake us. But, He leaves the decision to us. Will we leave *Him*? Will we forsake *Him*? Will we go off on our own path, apart from Him?

As we learned yesterday, we have the assurance that God, our Father, never changes. Additionally, we are promised that, "Jesus Christ is the same yesterday and today and forever," (Hebrews 13:8). If we choose to follow Him and walk on His path, the Bible tells us just where to start: by believing in Jesus Christ, His Son, who never changes, for He is the way to God. When we believe that Jesus is the Son of God, our example, and our Savior, that belief puts our feet on solid ground. The unchanging nature of Jesus provides a sure foundation for our feet.

If we want to walk the path of our lives with God, we must begin by stepping out on the foundation He has laid.

Do you know the way to the Father?

Isaiah 28:16 (NLT); John 14:6; Acts 4:12

Day Three

And now, dear children, remain in fellowship with Christ so that when he returns, you will be full of courage and not shrink back from him in shame.

1 John 2:28 (NLT)

If we desire to walk with God throughout our lives, we will choose the sure and solid path, whose foundation is Jesus. He is the way to the Father. He is our solid ground. What will put our feet on that solid ground is having a *believing* relationship with Jesus and accepting Him as our Lord and Savior. Through this foundational belief, we receive forgiveness for the sin and wrong in our lives, and we receive the gift of eternal life in heaven at the end of our earthly lives.

This foundational belief in Jesus secures our *eternal* life, but what about the here and now? God willing, we have a long path of life to walk on earth before we reach our heavenly home, so what is going to keep us on solid ground as we walk that path? The answer lies in 1 John 2:28: continuing to live in fellowship with Jesus. This means that we need to advance our relationship with Jesus from a *believing* relationship to a personal one.

Many of us have chosen to make Jesus the foundation of our lives. Much more is needed if we want to walk with Him throughout our lives. Jesus calls us *friend*, and He desires to have a personal relationship with us.

How can you make Jesus your friend?

John 15:14; 1 Corinthians 1:9

Day Four

I am the good shepherd; I know my sheep and my sheep know me.

John 10:14

Jesus is so intimately acquainted with all of our ways. He knows us inside and out. He has even numbered every hair on our heads. Jesus *knows* us. We have a tendency to only know Jesus on the surface. We think that because He is so mighty and powerful and all-knowing that we could not possibly have more than a believing relationship with Him. In other words, our relationship with Jesus tends to consist of us believing in Him. Period. Nothing more.

But John 10:14 tells us that our relationship with Jesus is meant to be so much more. We, as Jesus' followers — his sheep — are to *know* Him, not merely believe in Him. Sheep quickly come to know their shepherd as one who will lead them and guide them. By being in the shepherd's abiding presence, they learn about him and know that he always has their best interests in mind. They learn to listen for his voice, knowing that they will be safe and secure when they follow after him. Likewise, Jesus wants us to know Him as our Shepherd — as one who will lead and guide us. He wants us to learn about Him and trust that He will always have our best interests in mind. A sheep comes to trust in and follow after its shepherd when it *knows* him. A friend comes to trust in and follow after another friend when he *knows* him. Jesus wants us to *know* Him. He wants to be our friend. He desires a close, intimate, *personal* relationship with us.

How well do you know Jesus?

Psalm 139:1; Matthew 10:30; John 17:3

Day Five

My sheep listen to my voice; I know them, and they follow
me.

John 10:27

We are told in the Word that we can, and should, pray about everything. We are told that the Lord bends down to hear our every prayer. Jesus listens when we speak, but a friendship is not just about one person being the speaker and the other being the listener. A friendship exists when both freely speak and actively listen to one another.

How does Jesus speak to us? He may speak in a voice that we sense in our hearts or deep down in our spirits. He always speaks to us through the Bible, which is His ever-present voice to us. He may speak to us through a godly friend. The way that we come to recognize His voice, and how He speaks specifically to us, is in the consistent *listening*. In other words, as we come to Him continuously throughout the day in prayer, seeking His will as we go about our day, we begin to see His answer to our prayers. As He sees our faith and trust in Him by consistent prayer, He begins to reveal more of Himself to us. We begin to realize that He *does* speak to us, all we have to do is listen and learn to recognize His voice.

In Revelation 3:20, Jesus says to us, "Look! Here I stand

at the door and knock. If you hear me calling and open the door, I will come in, and we will share a meal as friends." (NLT) Jesus speaks to us—in our spirits, through His Word, and through our friends. He knocks on the door of our hearts with His voice, longing to share Himself with one who dares to listen.

Can you keep your heart open so that you may hear His voice?

Psalm 116:1–2 (NLT); 1 Thessalonians 5:17

Deuteronomy 30:20; Mark 9:7

Day Six

... let the wise listen and add to their learning, and let the discerning get guidance ...

Proverbs 1:5

When we develop a friendship with someone, we desire and strive to know more about him or her. The same should be true in our friendship with Jesus. He knows us so well; therefore, if we truly desire to develop a personal relationship with Him, we should desire and strive to know more about *Him*.

If we want to learn more about Jesus, the best place to start is prayer. Praying about everything leads us to this wonderful, ongoing fellowship with Jesus — as long as we are taking the time to listen to Him, as well. If we want to learn more about Jesus, we should take advantage of every opportunity to do so through church attendance, Christian events, and Bible studies. Whenever we have the opportunity to hear about Jesus then we have the opportunity to learn more about Him.

A transforming moment in my life occurred when I was reading the 139th Chapter of Psalms. I'd read it before, but this time it really spoke to me. Jesus *knew* me. He created me. He knew me before I was born on this earth, and He knows the day I will take my last breath on this earth. That opened my eyes to the fact that Jesus had not only a personal knowledge of me, but I was created for a specific purpose on this earth. Learning this about Jesus has led me to develop that personal relationship that He was longing to have with me. It has led me to trust in Him to fulfill His purpose in my life, and not make my own way. Learning about Jesus is essential to transforming our relationship with Him from merely a believing one to a personal one.

What opportunities are you taking to add to your learning about Jesus?

Proverbs 9:9; Proverbs 23:12; Colossians 1:10 (NLT)

Day Seven

Your word is a lamp to my feet and a light for my path.

Psalm 119:105

Ah, the Bible, the Word of God. We tend to be so intimidated by it. For some of us, it seems so hard to understand that we convince ourselves we never will. And so, we content ourselves with hearing it only as it is read to us by our pastors, teachers, and leaders. Oh, how I can relate! My Bible sat neatly on my bookshelf, in pristine condition because it was never used. When I was expecting my children, I took it off the shelf and read what I thought were the easier-to-understand books — Psalms and Proverbs. When I was thirty years old, I was asked to teach Sunday school to first and second graders. Thankfully, I was filled with a desire to know a bit more about what I was teaching. That desire led me to my neatly-shelved Bible, and instead of going straight to Psalms and Proverbs, I started at the very beginning in Genesis.

All too often, we tend to have a second-hand knowledge of the Bible. We hear it as it is read or taught to us, but we don't take the time to read it for ourselves. I am so glad I was asked to teach because it made me realize I had so much to learn myself! Reading the Bible for myself was crucial to developing a personal relationship with Jesus. It helped me see who Jesus really is and all of the many ways I needed Him — not just for eternal life, but in every day of my life. It helped me learn *how* to follow after Jesus. The Bible is a lamp that illuminates Jesus to us, so we may know Him. The Bible is a light that reveals His path to us so that we may walk in it.

The desire to learn more about Jesus should lead us straight to the Word of God. We will not always understand what we read, but as He sees our faithfulness in reading His Word, He will increase our understanding of what we are reading. His Word will truly illuminate our path if we will open it up and use its light.

How is God's Word a lamp for *your* feet and a light for *your* path?

Matthew 4:4; James 1:25

Day Eight

You will seek me and find me when you seek me with all your heart.

Jeremiah 29:13

We have been talking about developing our friendship with Jesus by learning more about Him. Our salvation requires that we simply believe in Jesus and what He did for us on the cross. Actually having a friendship — a personal relationship — with Jesus requires more from us. This means that we are going to have to work at it. We are going to have to work to not only pray to Him about everything, but learn to listen for His voice in our lives, as well. Likewise, we are going to have to work to discipline ourselves to not let our feelings of fear or intimidation stop us from reading His Word.

The Bible tells us of Ezra, "a teacher well versed in the Law of Moses, which the LORD, the God of Israel, had given" (Ezra 7:6). So this was a man who knew God's Word — so well, in fact, that he was able to teach it to others. A hidden gem is found in verse 10 that helps us see why Ezra knew God's Word so well: "For Ezra had *devoted himself* to the study and observance of the Law of the LORD, and to teaching its decrees and laws in Israel" (emphasis mine). Ezra's heart was not naturally drawn to the reading and studying of God's

Word. Ezra had to *devote himself* to it. He had to decide in his heart that he wanted to learn more about God, and then he had to work at it. He found God because he sought after Him with all his heart.

Can you do the same?

Psalm 119:30; Psalm 119:36; Proverbs 4:4

Day Nine

For these commands are a lamp, this teaching is a light, and the corrections of discipline are the way to life.

Proverbs 6:23

This path we call life is hard! There are twists and turns all along the way. There are stumbling blocks that trip us, temptations that lure us, and darkness that blinds us. Yet, God tells us that His Word is *a lamp* and *a light* for that path. The Bible is not simply a book of ancient history, but a Book that is full of current and relevant application for today and throughout the future. It provides hope. It comforts, teaches, guides, and corrects. If we want to know God more, there is no better way than looking into the very Words that He inspired.

> Most of all, you must understand this: No prophecy in the Scriptures ever comes from the prophet's own interpretation. No prophecy ever came from what a person wanted to say, but people led by the Holy Spirit spoke words from God.
>
> —2 Peter 1:20–21 (NCV)

God speaks to us through His Word. If you want to walk the path of life with God, open His Word and let His *lamp* and His *light* guide you.

Are you walking in the light of God's presence?

Psalm 119:35 (NLT); 2 Timothy 3:16–17; Hebrews 4:12

Day Ten

Listen, my son, and be wise, and keep your heart on the right path.

Proverbs 23:19

We learned earlier that if we desire to walk with God throughout our lives, we need to choose the sure and solid path, with Jesus as our foundation or solid ground. We learned that, in order to stay on that solid ground, we need to develop a closer, more personal relationship with Jesus. Developing a personal relationship with Jesus requires that we learn more about Him. As we learn more about Him, (through praying, listening, reading His Word), we see the example He gave us to follow and we learn the way He wants us to live our lives.

And now, what determines whether or not we stay on solid ground is what we do with what we see and learn of Jesus. We can't simply settle for reading the Word of God and seeing the example of Jesus. Instead, we need to *use* the Word of God, applying it to how we live our lives. Over and over in the Word of God, we see how Jesus lived His earthly life as an example of how we should live *our* earthly lives. God made Jesus to be our example because His ultimate goal for our lives is that we become more like Him.

James 1:22; 1 Peter 2:21

Day Eleven

And all of us have had that veil removed so that we can be
mirrors that brightly reflect the glory of the Lord.

2 Corinthians 3:18a (NLT)

The Book of Exodus describes the life of Moses, a man called by God to be His spokesperson to the people of Israel. Moses climbed to the top of Mt. Sinai to meet with God. After spending those times with God on top of the mountain, Moses' face was radiant as he came back down to the people. By being in the presence of God, Moses' face caught a reflection of the beauty and splendor — the glory — of God. That reflection of God's glory caused Moses' face to shine. The Israelites would see the radiance of Moses' face each time he returned from speaking with the LORD, so they knew that Moses was a representative of God. But after a time away from the LORD's presence, that radiance would fade from Moses' face. Because Moses did not want the Israelites to see that radiance fading away, Moses would put a veil over his face until the next time he spoke with God. He would remove the veil whenever he was in God's presence.

Moses reflected God's glory from being in His Presence and beholding, or looking to Him. As believers, we, too, can reflect God's glory by being in His presence and beholding, or looking to Him. God's glory is in His Word — the mirror through which we can see the glory of the LORD and behold Him. God's Word *reflects* Jesus to us. When we look into His Word, we reflect His Glory because to look to Jesus has a transforming power. Just as 2 Corinthians 3:18 promises, when we look upon Jesus, we become more like Him.

Will you look into God's Word and allow Him to reflect His glory through you?

Exodus 34:29; 2 Corinthians 3:11–13 & 16

Day Twelve

My son, if you accept my words and store up my commands within you, turning your ear to wisdom and applying your heart to understanding, and if you call out for insight and cry aloud for understanding, and if you look for it as for silver and search for it as for hidden treasure, then you will understand the fear of the LORD and find the knowledge of God.

Proverbs 2:1–5

As I mentioned in the Introduction, God awakened a hunger and thirst in me to know Him more. This came about when I was preparing to teach Sunday school for the first time. God prompted me to try to learn more about Him for myself by reading His Word from the beginning. Before long, I had formed a discipline for reading the Bible every day, which developed into a craving to read it every day, which has not left me. Did I understand all I was reading? Of course not. But God saw that I was seeking Him. He saw that I desired to know Him more, and He began to reveal more of Himself to me, just as He promises in the above verse. He saw that I was "turning [my] ear to wisdom and applying [my] heart to understanding," and, from there I began to "find the knowledge of God."

All too often we tend to settle for taking the word of

our teachers, pastors, and leaders *only* instead of seeking to make it personal. This comes about as a result of not seeking to know Him beyond the walls of the church. Advancing our relationship with Jesus from merely a believing one to a personal one requires that we carve out daily, alone time with Him for prayer and for reading His Word. That's when He's really going to reveal Himself to us and help us know Him more personally.

How much of your day is spent alone with Jesus?

Psalm 119:27 (NLT); James 1:5

Day Thirteen

But if from there you seek the LORD your God, you will find him if you look for him with all your heart and with all your soul.

Deuteronomy 4:29

I have spent much time speaking about the Word of God because it *is* the Word of God that led me to this amazing discovery of Who He really is and how very much of Him I was missing in my life. It all begins with seeking Him for ourselves—with all our heart and all our soul. Not sure where to begin? A great starting place is looking into the verses listed at the end of each daily devotional. As you read the verses in your Bible, spend time meditating on them. Ask God to give you insight into how you can apply theses verses personally in your own life.

The concordance at the back of the Bible is a valuable tool for reading and learning God's Word. The concordance lists many words with corresponding Biblical references. Looking up the references for a specific word leads us right to what God has to say about that word or subject. I continually take advantage of the concordance and find that it has helped me learn more about God and His Word. Another thing that has helped me gain a better understanding of the Word of God is in reading the same verses in different translations. We need to find, and read, the translation that helps us understand God's Word in the best way for us. The most important thing is that we *seek* Him.

Can you say that you are seeking Him with all your heart and soul?

Psalm 119:2; Proverbs 8:17

Day Fourteen

Now you've got my feet on the life path, all radiant from the shining of your face. Ever since you took my hand, I'm on the right way.

Psalm 16:11 (MSG)

Reading God's Word opens us up to an entirely new level of *relationship* with Him. Before, as we heard His Word read to us by our pastors, teachers, and leaders, we learned about God superficially. Now, upon disciplining ourselves to read the Word personally and privately with Him, every fiber of our being is ready to know Him deeply and intimately. As we read His Word, we are more closely in tune to how He speaks to us through it. We have the Bible as our personal guidebook on how to navigate through this life and keep on the path He intends for us. God's Word reflects Jesus to us, allowing us, then, to reflect Him to others.

Reading God's Word opens us up to an entirely new level of *communication* with Him. We see that His Word is filled with His promises, and that not one of His promises has ever been broken (see Joshua 23:14). So now, as we read His Word for ourselves, we may pray His Word back to Him. For example, we may pray, "Lord, Your Word says that if I confess my sins to You, You are 'faithful and just' to forgive me (see 1 John 1:9); so, Lord, 'do as you promised,' (see 2

2 Samuel 7:25), and forgive me."

Remember, God's Word is a lamp for our feet and a light for our path (see Psalm 119:105 and Day Seven). We just need to open it, read it, and use it.

Numbers 23:19; 2 Peter 1:3–5 (NLT)

Day Fifteen

If you love me, obey my commandments. And I will ask the Father, and he will give you another Counselor, who will never leave you. He is the Holy Spirit, who leads into all truth.

John 14:15–17a (NLT)

What are we going to do with what we see and learn of Jesus? Are we going to obey? Are we going to do what we see and learn to do as we look to Jesus' example? Jesus knows this is the hard part, so He provides help for us, as promised in the above verses. That help comes in the form of the Holy Spirit. How do we get the Holy Spirit? That question is answered in Ephesians:

> And now you also have heard the truth, the Good News that God saves you. And when you believed in Christ, he identified you as his own by giving you the Holy Spirit, whom he promised long ago. The Spirit is God's guarantee that he will give us everything he promised and that he has purchased us to be his own people. This is just one more reason for us to praise our glorious God. (Ephesians 1:13–14, NLT)

This means that at the very moment that we believe in Jesus as our Savior — at that *very* moment of belief — He sends the Holy Spirit to live within us. Indeed, that *is* "just one more reason for us to praise our glorious God!"

Acts 2:38–39 (NLT); 2 Corinthians 1:20–22

Day Sixteen

And this expectation will not disappoint us. For we know how dearly God loves us, because he has given us the Holy Spirit to fill our hearts with his love.

Romans 5:5 (NLT)

God loved us so much that He sent Jesus to this earth as flesh and blood to live among us. Throughout His earthly life, Jesus was well acquainted with struggles. He knows the challenges that we face in this life, especially if we choose to walk with Him. That is why we are given the Holy Spirit—to fill our hearts with His great love for us, and to help us walk our life path with Him.

The Holy Spirit is our Comforter, our Counselor, and our Guide as we navigate through this life. The Holy Spirit fills our hearts with the love of God, reassuring us that we are never alone. Take a minute to let that soak in—*you are never alone!* The Holy Spirit speaks to the Father for us when we have no words to say ourselves. The Holy Spirit increases our understanding of God and His Word, and helps us know Him more. The Holy Spirit, quite literally, shows us what is God's will and way for our lives. Jesus comforted His disciples with these words about the coming Holy Spirit:

But when the Friend comes, the Spirit of the Truth, he will take you by the hand and guide you into all the truth there is. He won't draw attention to himself, but will make sense out of what is about to happen and, indeed, out of all that I have done and said. He will honor me; he will take from me and deliver it to you. John 16:13–14 (MSG)

Praise God for His most precious Holy Spirit!

Joshua 1:9; Romans 8:26 (NLT)

John 14:26; John 15:26 (NLT)

Day Seventeen

Christ died for all so that those who live would not continue to live for themselves. He died for them and was raised from the dead so that they would live for him.

2 Corinthians 5:15 (NCV)

We've just learned that at the very moment we believe in Jesus, He sends His Spirit to come and live in our hearts. But you may think, "I never knew the Holy Spirit lived in me! I don't feel any differently. I didn't know I had Someone to guide me and help me understand more about God and His Word." And I will say that I know just how you might feel because I have experienced those same feelings myself. And, I know *why* now. We may *know* that we are saved because we prayed a prayer stating that we believe in Jesus and what He did for us on the cross. I remember the day I prayed that prayer when I was about eight or nine years old, standing in the backyard with my next door neighbor, a preacher's daughter, leading me in prayer. Why do I remember it so clearly? I remember it because it was sincere. I truly believe that is the day I received forgiveness of my sins and eternal life in heaven.

Why, then, did I spend the next twenty-two years or so of my life neither feeling nor living differently than I had *before* I had prayed that prayer, yet knowing that my sins were forgiven and I was going to heaven when my earthly life was over? It was because I had that *believing* relationship with Jesus, but nothing more. I *believed* in Him, which put me on solid ground. But, I didn't do anything to *develop* my relationship with Him. Therefore, I spent the next twenty-two years wandering off the path, getting back on, wandering off, and then getting back on again. Quite simply, I was continuing to live for myself. Jesus died and was raised back to life so that we, as believers, would live our lives for *Him*.

Romans 6:12–13 (NLT); Romans 12:1 (NLT)

Day Eighteen

If anyone belongs to Christ, there is a new creation. The old things have gone; everything is made new!

2 Corinthians 5:17 (NCV)

In this verse, God is saying that once we accept Jesus as our Lord and Savior, we belong to Him. He wants us to leave our old, self-centered ways behind and become "a new creation" — to live for Him. This is what it means to belong to Jesus. What is this new creation like? The new creation is a changed life, because as we surrender ourselves to Jesus, we become more like Him and less like our old selves. God wants our salvation to *change* us. Listen to His words from Ezekiel:

> I'll pour pure water over you and scrub you clean. I'll give you a new heart, put a new spirit in you. I'll remove the stone heart from your body and replace it with a heart that's God-willed, not self-willed. I'll put my Spirit in you and make it possible for you to do what I tell you and live by my commands. (Ezekiel 36:25–27, MSG)

Once we ask Jesus to come and live in our hearts, we do indeed receive forgiveness for our sins. As promised in the above verses from Ezekiel, God cleanses us and replaces our old, self-centered heart with a new, God-centered one. He sends His Spirit to live in us and make it possible to live this new, God-centered life. But in order for that to happen, something very significant is required of us: our repentance. What that means is that, unless we choose to turn away from our old sins and surrender to Him, *nothing* will change inside of us.

Are you willing to put God in the center of your life and take yourself out? This is the key to becoming the new creation God desires you to be.

Romans 8:12–13 (NCV; MSG)

Colossians 3:3–4 (NCV)

Day Nineteen

Yet, O LORD, you are our Father. We are the clay, you are the potter; we are all the work of your hand.

Isaiah 64:8

Before a potter can transform a lump of clay into a marvelous masterpiece, he must first make sure that the lump of clay can be molded. The first step is making sure that the clay is in the right place on the potter's wheel. Otherwise, the clay will be wobbly and off-balanced. It will move around without any clear direction, which will not allow the potter to take hold of it and mold it. The clay has to be of the right consistency. If it's too hard or too soft, the potter will not be able to mold it and shape it into what he desires. It is only when the clay has met these requirements that it can be used by the potter and transformed from a lump into a masterpiece.

Knowing this gives us a better understanding of the above verse from Isaiah. As our Creator, God has a plan for each of us that He longs to fulfill. The fulfillment of His plan for us requires that we, like clay, meet the requirements needed to be used and transformed by our Potter. That means that we stay within His will, or plan, for our lives, and that we *surrender* to that will. We do so when we put God at the very center of our lives. Our center is what we spend most of our time thinking about and doing. Whatever our center is influences what we think, say, and do. It is only right and fitting that our Creator would want to be the One influencing what we think, say, and do.

God is our Potter, we are His clay. He desires to make us into His marvelous masterpiece, but, in order for Him to do so, we must make *Him* the center of our lives. Only then will we be prepared to follow His lead and do His will.

Have you made God the center of your life?

Isaiah 45:9 (NLT); Jeremiah 18:6

Day Twenty

And as the Spirit of the Lord works within us, we become more and more like him and reflect his glory even more.

2 Corinthians 3:18b (NLT)

Back on Day Eleven, we learned that Moses' face literally glowed after he had been in the presence of God. Why did his face glow? Because, spending time in God's presence caused God's glory — His beauty and splendor — to be reflected in the face of Moses. For us, God's glory can be seen on every page of His Word. His Word reflects His perfect Son, Jesus, to us. Therefore, when we look into that Word, *we* are then enabled to reflect His glory. That is what is meant in the first part of the verse:

> And all of us have had that veil removed so that
> we can be mirrors that brightly reflect the glory
> of the Lord. (2 Corinthians 3:18, NLT)

God's Word reflects Jesus to us. As we read His Word, we are then able to reflect Him to others. This is what we were put on this earth to do: reflect Jesus to others. In fact, God's ultimate goal for us is that we become more like Jesus. The second part of 2 Corinthians 3:18 spells out what is necessary in order for us to reflect Jesus even more — the Holy Spirit working within us. The Holy Spirit works within us when we put God in the center of our lives and yield ourselves to His will, living in obedience to Him instead of living for ourselves.

John 14:15–17; Acts 5:32

Day Twenty-One

So I advise you to live according to your new life in the Holy Spirit. Then you won't be doing what your sinful nature craves.

Galatians 5:16 (NLT)

This verse brings it all home: our salvation is supposed to *change* us. That is why, upon our believing in Jesus and what He did for us on the cross, God sends His Holy Spirit to dwell within us — to change us and offer us this new life. We have this new life available to us, but it is found only when we live *according to* the Holy Spirit. That means that we must live in the way that the Holy Spirit leads us, we must be in agreement with Him. You see, our *flesh* — that sinful part of us — will always think, say, and do the opposite of what the Holy Spirit wants us to think, say, and do:

> The old sinful nature loves to do evil, which is
> just opposite from what the Holy Spirit wants.
> And the Spirit gives us desires that are opposite
> from what the sinful nature desires. These two
> forces are constantly fighting each other, and
> your choices are never free from this conflict.
> (Galatians 5:17, NLT)

That is why it is so important that we live *according to* the leading of the Holy Spirit. The change, the new life, will come about when we are ready and willing to leave behind our old life, which was ruled by sin, and live in obedience to the Holy Spirit.

Have you left your old life behind?

Ephesians 4:22–24; 1 Peter 1:2 (MSG)

Day Twenty-Two

So, my brothers and sisters, we must not be ruled by our sinful selves or live the way our sinful selves want. If you use your lives to do the wrong things your sinful selves want, you will die spiritually. But if you use the Spirit's help to stop doing the wrong things you do with your body, you will have true life.

Romans 8:12–13 (NCV)

When we follow after the desires of our flesh, we're led to do the opposite of what the Holy Spirit would lead us to do. On our own, we are *inclined* to do wrong—that is our sinful nature. This is why Jesus asks the Father to send His Holy Spirit to dwell within us—to help us, to counsel us between right and wrong, and to lead us to do what is right.

Paul, the very author of the words above, underwent a most dramatic transformation when he believed in Jesus and received the Holy Spirit. He was once a fanatic, bent on preventing the work of Jesus' disciples. Then one day, Jesus appeared to him in a light so bright it left him blind for three days. Afterward, his sight was restored, and he was filled with the Holy Spirit. The Spirit worked in Paul's life and transformed him from a self-centered, evil man to one of Jesus' most faithful followers who dedicated his life to sharing Jesus with others (see Acts 9). By yielding to the Holy Spirit within him, Paul was transformed into the godly man God desired him to be.

What exactly does the Holy Spirit do, and how does He do it? Well, first and foremost, since the Holy Spirit dwells within us, we will experience His counsel *internally*. We will feel the Holy Spirit's counsel within our minds, teaching us truth, helping us know right from wrong, sinful from godly. We will feel the Holy Spirit's counsel within our spirits, convicting us when we do wrong, leading us to repent, or turn away from our wrong and seek forgiveness.

The Holy Spirit lives within us as a Helper, a Counselor, and a guide for walking our life's path with God. What could be better?

John 16:13; John 16:8

Day Twenty-Three

So give yourselves completely to God. Stand against the devil, and the devil will run from you. Come near to God, and God will come near to you.

James 4:7–8a (NCV)

We have learned that the *flesh*, or sinful part, of our nature will always want to say and do the opposite of what the Holy Spirit will want us to say and do. Galatians 5:17 says that these are two "forces" that are constantly at war, and that in every choice we make we'll face this conflict. It's like the symbolism of the devil on one shoulder and the angel on the other shoulder — both trying to direct us. What are we to do? James 4:7 tells us: We are to give ourselves completely to God and stand against, or resist, the devil, or Satan.

Just how do we do this? This is where we can really tap into the help of the Holy Spirit. Remember, one of the "jobs" of the Holy Spirit is to counsel us, to help us know right from wrong. So often we tend to think, speak, and act completely on our own. This is just what Satan loves for us to do. But if we are to let our salvation change us, we will allow the Holy Spirit to work in us and counsel us so that we are no longer living a life led by our flesh, or by Satan, but one led by the Holy Spirit. This will mean that — instead of thinking, speaking, and acting on our own — we will first seek the counsel of the Holy Spirit through prayer. Satan loves when we act on our own, but resisting this urge is taking a stand against him.

Giving ourselves completely to God means that we seek His will in all that we do and resist Satan's temptations to act on our own. The Holy Spirit will always lead us to do the will of God. All we have to do is pray for His leading.

John 16:15 (NLT); 1 Peter 5:8–9

Day Twenty-Four

For all have sinned; all fall short of God's glorious standard.
Romans 3:23 (NLT)

What happens when we reject the counsel of the Holy Spirit? What if we feel Him leading us to do or not do something, but instead of following that leading, we do what our flesh desires? Quite simply, we sin. What is sin? Sin is wrongdoing. Sin is going against the will of God. Romans 3:23 reminds us that none of us is without sin in our lives. But if the Holy Spirit dwells in us, we will experience another wonderful benefit: conviction. You see, another job of the Holy Spirit is to serve as our conscience, causing us to feel guilt when we have done wrong.

The Holy Spirit does not convict us of our sins so that we will feel guilt that will lead us to condemnation and hopelessness. Instead, the Holy Spirit convicts us so that we will feel guilt that will lead us straight to the throne of God, asking for and receiving His forgiveness. God will always know what we have done wrong, but He wants us to know our wrong as well. That is the purpose of conviction: to help us know our wrong, and feel the guilt and sorrow over that wrong, so that we will seek God's forgiveness.

Satan desires for us to feel just the opposite. He wants us to feel condemned and unworthy of God's forgiveness so that we are too hopeless to even seek that forgiveness. But God's Word speaks truth to us: There is no condemnation, and we may always come boldly to God, seeking and *finding* His forgiveness.

Romans 8:1; Hebrews 4:16 (NLT)

Day Twenty-Five

But the Counselor, the Holy Spirit, whom the Father will send in my name, will teach you all things and will remind you of everything I have said to you.

John 14:26

Yet another job of the Holy Spirit is to teach us and remind us of the things that Jesus said to us when He lived here on earth. In other words, the Holy Spirit will help us gain an understanding of all that is contained in the Word of God. We learned way back on Day Seven that though we may not understand all that we are reading in the Bible, if we are faithful *in* our reading, God will increase our understanding of *what* we are reading. God accomplishes this work through His Holy Spirit.

Our role in this is to remain faithful in reading His Word. Once we decide to *devote* ourselves to the reading and studying of God's Word (see Day Eight), the promised Holy Spirit will begin to open our eyes and give us enlightenment and understanding of what we are reading and studying. It is our job to become sensitive to His leading, His teaching, and His guiding, and then to act in obedience *to* that leading, teaching, and guiding. The more we follow His leading, the more we will be led by Him.

Psalm 119:104; Proverbs 3:5; Ephesians 4:30a (NLT)

Day Twenty-Six

If your sinful nature controls your mind, there is death. But if the Holy Spirit controls your mind, there is life and peace.

Romans 8:6 (NLT)

When we allow the Holy Spirit to control our minds, we live according to His counsel. What this means is that we will seek His will in what we think, say, and do, and obey what He *leads* us to think, say, and do. This also means that, when we feel Him convicting us of our sins, we will stop sinning and seek God's forgiveness. This is what it means to allow the Holy Spirit to control our minds. This will help us to live our lives in a way that is pleasing to the Lord.

But, as we learned on Day Twenty, we were put on this earth for even more. We were put on this earth to reflect Jesus to others. When we allow the Holy Spirit to control our minds, we will receive yet another benefit from Him: He will help us reflect Jesus even more. You see, when we allow the Holy Spirit to control our minds, our lives will begin to show *evidence* that He is in control. That evidence comes in the form of "fruit" that the Holy Spirit produces in us. It is in that fruit that others are enabled to see Jesus in us.

Jesus calls us to bear fruit. He wants our lives to show others that we love and follow after Him. In this, we are able to reflect Jesus and lead others to Him.

Can others see Jesus in you?

John 15:16a; John 15:8

Day Twenty-Seven

I am the vine; you are the branches. If a man remains in me and I in him, he will bear much fruit; apart from me you can do nothing.

John 15:5

If we were to pluck the branches off of a vine, could those branches exist, could they be useful? The answer is no, they could not, because they would have no source of nutrients and nothing that would sustain them or keep them alive. The same is true of us attempting to exist and be useful apart from Jesus. John 15:5 tells us that apart from Jesus, we can do *nothing*. He is our Source of life; He is the Source of our fruitfulness, our usefulness. As we learned yesterday, Jesus calls us to bear fruit in our lives. He desires for our lives to show evidence that we love and follow after Him. This is what it means to "bear fruit."

But, just as branches separated from the vine could not be fruitful and grow apart from the vine, so our lives cannot be fruitful and reflect Jesus apart from Him. Jesus wants us to bear fruit in order to glorify God, so that He, the Source of all that is good, is honored and praised. Jesus wants us to bear fruit as evidence that we love and follow after Him. In this way, our lives will reflect Jesus to others, just as they should.

This is the why, now what about the how? How do we

remain in Jesus? It's in maintaining that close, intimate, *personal* relationship with Him in praying and listening to Him. It's in reading and studying His Word — the "lamp" and "light" for our path. Remaining close to Jesus provides the nutrient-rich Source that will allow us to "go and bear fruit."

Jeremiah 17:7–8; Colossians 1:10

Day Twenty-Eight

Watch out for false prophets. They come to you in sheep's clothing, but inwardly they are ferocious wolves. By their fruit you will recognize them.

Matthew 7:15–16a

In Jesus' time on earth, false prophets existed. A prophet is a special messenger sent by God to warn people, or give them a special message that God has spoken to the prophet. Therefore, a false prophet is one who gives a message or warning that he *pretends* is from God. We have false prophets aplenty today. Among today's false prophets is every person who calls himself a Christian but doesn't show it in how he or she speaks and acts. Another word for this type of false prophet is a hypocrite. In the above verse, Jesus shares with us how we can recognize such a false prophet: "by their fruit."

If *fruit* is evidence, then please know that there can be bad fruit, as well as good fruit. That means that the fruit that people bear — their words and their actions, and how they live their lives — will help us recognize whether or not they are truly Christ-followers/Christians who bear spiritual fruit, or whether they are hypocrites who follow their sinful flesh. The same is true for us. What kind of evidence do we show in our lives that points to the fact that we love and follow after Jesus?

Do our words and actions reflect humility, holiness, and love? Or do our words and actions reflect pride, worldliness, and division?

Again, we must remain in Jesus if are to bear the good fruit that reflects Him to others.

John 15:4; James 3:17

Day Twenty-Nine

Then he told them many things in parables, saying: "A farmer went out to sow his seed ..."

Matthew 13:3

In Matthew 13, Jesus tells the parable, or story-with-a-lesson, about a farmer who went out to plant his seed. As the farmer plants his seed, some of it falls in places that the farmer did not intend for it to fall. In each of these places, the seed is not fruitful — it either doesn't grow at all, or it doesn't continue to grow. As Jesus tells this story about the farmer, His lesson is this: not everyone who hears the message about Jesus will allow it to be *implanted* and become *fruitful* in their lives.

Colossians 1:10 tells us that the way to please the Lord is by "bearing fruit in every good work," and by "growing in the knowledge of God." By this verse we know that God wants us to continually grow in our learning of Him, and He wants our lives to continually bear fruit, or show evidence, that we love and follow after Him. In this parable, the seed represents the Word of God, and where it falls represents the way that we respond to His Word. How and where this seed is planted is vital to its growing and bearing fruit. This Parable of the Sower is a powerful message to us that we must take care how we hear and respond to God's Word.

Psalm 119:11; Matthew 15:13

Day Thirty

As he was scattering the seed, some fell along the path, and the birds came and ate it up.

Matthew 13:4

Imagine the farmer walking along a path, heading for his garden. He's carrying all his seed, and as he walks along the path to the garden, some of that seed falls from his load and is scattered along the pathway. What happens to that seed? The birds come and eat it up.

Remember that, in this parable, the seed represents the Word of God, and where it falls represents the way that we respond to that Word. Jesus explains that the seed that fell along the path and was eaten up by the birds represents those who hear the message about Him but don't understand it. Instead of trying to learn and understand it, they just give up. The birds represent the devil, Jesus says, who comes and takes away what was planted in that person's heart. It's like hearing about Jesus, not getting it at all, and just giving up. Satan loves this because he just swoops in and takes away everything that the person heard.

It is so vital that we pray for the Holy Spirit to help us when we don't understand God's Word. His counsel is what we need to ensure that we are "growing in the knowledge of God" so that we can be "bearing fruit in every good work" (see Colossians 1:10). By our own strength and ability, we will never be able to fully understand the Word of God.

Matthew 13:19; Proverbs 2:6

Day Thirty-One

Some fell on rocky places, where it did not have much soil. It sprang up quickly, because the soil was shallow. But when the sun came up, the plants were scorched, and they withered because they had no root.

Matthew 13:5–6

As the farmer begins to sow his seed, some of it falls on ground that is rocky and shallow. When we plant a seed, we don't see evidence right away because the work first begins underneath the ground. The plant must first form a root system to supply the nutrients it needs to grow. The ground that this seed fell upon was rocky and very shallow. Because of this, the roots had no depth, so the plants sprang up very quickly. However, the lack of a healthy, deep root system did not allow the plants to get the nutrients they needed, so they dried up.

Jesus explains that this seed is like those who hear about Him and get very excited about it. But they don't let the teaching go deep into their lives. The excitement and joy they initially experienced fades away, and when some problem or difficulty arises, there is nothing to show for it because their belief was built on emotion and not allowed to go any deeper.

That is why it is so important that we *develop* our relationship with Jesus. We want our knowledge of Jesus to be deep and personal, not shallow and superficial. And then, as we "remain in" Him (see John 15:4), He will be the nutrient-rich Source we need to grow and be fruitful.

Matthew 13:20–21; 1 Corinthians 3:7

Day Thirty-Two

Other seed fell among thorns, which grew up and choked the plants.

Matthew 13:7

As the farmer was planting his seed, some of it fell among thorns and weeds. I need only to look at my own yard to understand what happened with this seed. As so often is the case, if we have any weeds or thorny sandspurs in our yard, these grow very quickly, only to choke out and overtake our healthy grass. This is what happened here with the farmer's seed. The thorns and weeds grew up and choked out the good plants from the farmer's seed, overtaking them.

Jesus says that this seed "is like the person who hears the teaching but lets worries about this life and the temptation of wealth stop that teaching from growing. So the teaching does not produce fruit in that person's life" (Matthew 13:22, NCV). I believe that this seed describes most of us: we let the cares of the world and the desire to get ahead overtake our relationship with Jesus.

We can't hear about Jesus and resume living like the world around us. It's where the rubber meets the road: Are we going to see and learn about Jesus and then just follow the ways of the world of "me first," or are we going to see and learn about Jesus and be *changed*? Are we actually going to live differently because we *know* Him now, and, because of that, *we know better?*

Matthew 13:22; John 15:19; James 4:4 (NLT)

Day Thirty-Three

Still other seed fell on good soil, where it produced a crop—a hundred, sixty or thirty times what was sown.

Matthew 13:8

At last we hear that some of the farmer's seed fell just where it was supposed to fall—on ground that had good soil. All of the conditions fell together to make this soil the most conducive for growing seed. What's more, this "good soil" caused the farmer's seed to grow abundantly—up to one hundred times the amount of the seed that he sowed.

Jesus explains that this seed "is like the person who hears the teaching and understands it. That person grows and produces fruit, sometimes a hundred times more, sometimes sixty times more, and sometimes thirty times more" (Matthew 13:23, NCV). This person understands God's Word because he takes the time to develop his relationship with Jesus. He takes the time to learn more about Him and follows the guidance of the Holy Spirit within him. And what happens? "That person grows and produces fruit ..."

The key to growing in God and producing fruit in our lives is *good soil*. That good soil is made up of a personal relationship with Jesus, and is nourished by a continuing obedience to the leading of the Holy Spirit.

Can we strive to let our lives be that good soil that will

allow us to grow and produce fruit?

Matthew 13:23; Psalm 1:1–3 (NLT)

Day Thirty-Four

Follow my example, as I follow the example of Christ.

1 Corinthians 11:1

On Day Twenty-Eight we learned that we as Christians are recognized by our fruit. Remember that bearing fruit is showing evidence in our lives that we love and follow after Jesus. As we have seen these last few days, God makes it very clear in His Word that He wants us to grow in our knowledge of Him and bear fruit, or show evidence, in our lives that we love and follow after Him. We learned yesterday that this requires a personal relationship with Jesus and obedience to the leading of the Holy Spirit.

What we must remember is that God calls us and enables us to bear fruit not to make *us* look good, but to point others to *Him*. In John 15:8, Jesus tells us that He wants us to "bear much fruit" so that we glorify, or honor, God and show ourselves to be His followers. Our fruit is what sets us apart as true, *word-and-action* Christians versus false, *word-only* hypocrites. That means that the evidence that we love and follow Jesus should be not just heard in our words, but seen in our actions, too. We must "walk our talk." Our fruit-bearing allows us to be a good example of what it means to be a Christ-follower. In our fruit-bearing, we are reflecting the Source of that fruit so that *He* gets the credit for our goodness.

And in our fruit-bearing, we are showing that we are who we claim to be — Christians, Christ-followers, people who love Jesus.

Being a Christ-follower will require us to have integrity — to be people who are true to our word. Being a Christ-follower means that Jesus is reflected not only in our words, but in our actions, too. As we follow the example of Christ, we become an *example* of Christ to others.

Matthew 7:20; 1 Timothy 4:12

Day Thirty-Five

One day as the crowds were gathering, Jesus went up the mountainside with his disciples and sat down to teach them.

Matthew 5:1 (NLT)

At this point in Jesus' ministry on earth, large crowds were continually following Him, to be healed by Him and to be taught by Him. On this particular day, as the crowds were gathering, Jesus climbed up a mountain with His disciples to teach them. The words that Jesus spoke to His followers are known as *The Beatitudes*, and part of Jesus' teaching widely referred to as The Sermon on the Mount.

In these *Beatitudes*, Jesus describes the character traits that all of His followers should have. Each of Jesus' statements begins with the words, "Blessed are ..." When we think of the word *blessed*, we think: joyful, fortunate, and set apart for good. The word *beatitude* actually means "supreme blessedness." Each of *The Beatitudes* is a statement that identifies the character trait that is blessed by God, followed by how they are to be blessed. Each of them includes a present blessing, "Blessed are," and a future blessing, "for theirs is," or "for they will."

To sum it up, *The Beatitudes* describe the traits that we, as Jesus' followers, should have. These traits set us apart from those who do not follow after Jesus, for God's desire for us is that we become more like Jesus and less like the world around us. Having these character traits is vital to growing and bearing fruit.

Are you ready to be "set apart?"

Leviticus 20:26; Romans 8:29 (NLT)

Day Thirty-Six

Blessed are the poor in spirit, for theirs is the kingdom of heaven.

Matthew 5:3

Jesus starts out by saying that those who are "poor in spirit" are blessed. They are joyful, fortunate, set apart for good. Now, when we think of the word *poor*, we think of being destitute, being without, being in need — not being joyful, fortunate, and set apart for good. But, let's consider what *poor in spirit* means. To be poor in spirit is to be completely humble in our own eyes. It is to look upon God and see that we are completely and utterly *nothing* before Him.

One who sees and recognizes that he is poor will take the steps needed to break free from his poverty. The same is true for the one who is poor in spirit. Once he sees and recognizes his poverty, he will take the steps needed to break free from his poverty. We are blessed when we are poor in spirit because we realize that we are nothing *before* God, but we also recognize that we are nothing *without* God. When we are poor in spirit, we recognize our need for God and depend on Him to lift us out of our spiritual poverty by filling us with *Him*. That is our present blessing. Our future blessing is that "the kingdom of heaven" will be ours. Our spiritual poverty draws us to God for our satisfaction, and our belief in Him leads us to eternal life in "the kingdom of heaven."

The world around us says we should look to our needs over and above anyone else's. The world around us values self-sufficiency and self-reliance. But Jesus says we should be poor in spirit, which means that we should not only be humble in our own eyes, but we should also realize our great need for and dependence upon God. Being poor in spirit means that we empty ourselves *of* ourselves, realizing our complete unworthiness apart from God.

James 4:10 (NLT); Romans 10:13

Day Thirty-Seven

Blessed are those who mourn ...

Matthew 5:4a

As we look into *The Beatitudes*, it is important to remember that Jesus used them to instruct His disciples *then*, and left this instruction for those of us who are His disciples, or followers, *today* to show us the people we ought to be. In this way, we will know what God expects of us, and what we can then expect from Him.

In the second *Beatitude*, Jesus calls us blessed for mourning. When we think of mourning, our first thought is usually that of grieving. Why would Jesus consider us to be blessed when we mourn? To answer that, it is important to know that *The Beatitudes* have nothing to do with our outer condition, but instead, our inner, or *spiritual*, condition. In this verse from Matthew, Jesus is not talking about mourning as we tend to know it. He is not talking about mourning over the loss of a loved one, or the loss of a job, or the loss of a home, or any other loss we may experience *outwardly* in this world. Instead, Jesus is referring to the internal, *spiritual*, mourning over sin.

We learned on Day Twenty-Four that one of the roles of the Holy Spirit is to convict us of our sins—to cause us to feel guilt and sorrow over them. The purpose for that conviction is to lead us to feel sorry for our sins and seek God's forgiveness. When we *mourn* over our sins, we are responding correctly to the Holy Spirit's conviction. In other words, we are allowing that conviction to cause us to be sorry for our sins so that we turn away from them (repent) and turn to God.

John 16:8; 2 Corinthians 7:10 (NCV)

Day Thirty-Eight

... for they will be comforted.

Matthew 5:4b

Being poor in spirit causes us to see our nothingness in comparison to God and motivates us to draw near to Him to lift us out of our spiritual poverty. In the same way, the deep anguish, grief, and sorrow experienced by "those who mourn" motivates us to draw near to God to seek a remedy for that mourning. The fact that we mourn, are deeply sorry for, *grieve* over, our sins is evidence that our consciences are now sensitive to the leading of the Holy Spirit within us. A sensitive conscience is going to feel conviction of even the slightest sin. For me, this has often meant conviction of prideful or judgmental thoughts. Although sinful thoughts seem innocent enough, they have the potential to go much deeper, becoming sinful words or actions. A conscience made sensitive by the Holy Spirit will feel remorse for sins that were once considered insignificant. What a gift that is, because that conviction is what will lead us to repent of—to turn away from—that sin and seek God's forgiveness and deliverance.

Jesus calls us blessed when we mourn because we are not only sorry for our sins, but we are drawn to the One Who can and will not only forgive us, but comfort us as well. We are blessed in the present because our sensitive consciences lead us away from our sins and straight to a God who will forgive us. We are blessed in the future when we enter our heavenly home and are in the presence of a God who will, quite literally, wipe every tear from our eyes.

2 Corinthians 1:3; Revelation 21:4

Day Thirty-Nine

Blessed are the meek, for they will inherit the earth.

Matthew 5:5

Looking to the third *Beatitude*, we see that Jesus considers those who are meek to be blessed. To be meek means to be humble, gentle, calm, and peaceful. Oftentimes, in the world's view, meekness is looked upon as being weak and submissive, being easily imposed upon. Instead of seeing meekness as a form of gentleness, the world sees it as a form of powerlessness. After all, meekness seems to go completely against the desire for power that is rampant in this world, a place where power is seen as a sign of success.

But meekness is a character trait that is very power*ful* in God's eyes. Just as in the world today, the people in biblical times took pride in their power and viewed it as a sign of success. Then along came Jesus who said, "Blessed are the meek …!" Jesus left us His example of One who is humble and gentle. Although humble and gentle, Jesus also showed examples of reacting with firmness when necessary (see Matthew 21:12–13, Matthew 23). You see, meekness is not weakness. Instead, meekness is being humble and obedient to God.

When we are meek, we have chosen to submit ourselves to God's will over our own. When we are meek, we are humble and don't think highly of ourselves, yet we are in no way weak. Instead, our humility and submission to God enable us to be completely balanced between gentleness and strength. Jesus calls blessed those who are meek. We are blessed *now* as we follow Jesus' example and become more like Him. We will be blessed *in the future* when we "inherit the earth," reigning with Him in His future kingdom on earth.

Matthew 11:29 (NLT); Psalm 37:11; Revelation 20:6 (NLT)

Day Forty

Blessed are those who hunger and thirst for righteousness ...
Matthew 5:6a

Jesus tells us in John 10:10 that He has come so that we could have a full, abundant life. He also tells us that Satan comes to take all of that away. You see, Satan would love nothing more than for us to never grow as Christians so that he can destroy the full and abundant life that Jesus came for us to have. Jesus wants us to grow in our knowledge of Him and bear fruit so that we will have a richer and fuller life — the one He died to give us.

In *The Beatitudes*, Jesus calls us blessed to have these characteristics because they will help us grow in our knowledge of Him, bear fruit for Him, and become more like Him. In the fourth *Beatitude*, Jesus calls "those who hunger and thirst for righteousness" blessed. We all know what it means to be hungry and thirsty, but to *hunger and thirst* goes deeper to describe an intense *craving*. Clearly, Jesus is not talking about us hungering and thirsting for food and drink here. Instead, He speaks about us having a hunger and thirst — an intense craving — for *righteousness*. Righteousness is living in a way that is obedient to God and the commands He gives us in His Word.

If we want to grow as Christians and live the abundant

life Jesus desires for us to have here and now on earth, then we will want to live out our faith and not just keep it inside. Our desire to grow and change will fill us with a hunger and thirst—an intense craving—for righteousness. Our desire to grow and change will fill us with a hunger and thirst—an intense craving—to live obediently to God. Our desire to grow and change will fill us with a hunger and thirst—an intense craving—for God to put us to work for *His* use here on earth. Our desire to grow and change will fill us with a hunger and thirst—an intense craving—to be more like Jesus.

John 10:10; Romans 6:12–13

Day Forty-One

... for they will be filled.

Matthew 5:6b

Someone who hungers and thirsts for righteousness does so not to gain the recognition of others, but out of an intense love for God and a desire to do what is right and pleasing to Him. Jesus tells us, in Matthew 6, not to worry about our lives but to seek God and His righteousness, and all of the things we need for our lives will then be provided to us. It's that same struggle we have in life between the world's view (our flesh), and God's view (our spirit). The world's view is to pursue our personal needs first and foremost, but God tells us to seek *Him* first, to seek after *righteousness*. And then, *He* will supply us with the other necessities of life.

Whether we realize it or not, we continually invite the world's views into our lives through what we hear and see on the radio, the Internet, in movies, and on TV, but what do we do to invite God's views into our lives? We need daily communication with Him in prayer and in His Word. And then we need to live out that daily communication with Him in obedience to what He tells us in His Word, through His Holy Spirit, and through whatever way we may hear Him speaking specifically to us in our lives.

Righteousness is obedience to God, and obedience is

the key to living the abundant life Jesus desires for us. When we hunger and thirst for the things of God, *He* will fill us. We will be blessed *now* as our intense craving for righteousness leads us to walk our talk and live obediently to God, becoming more like Jesus. We will be blessed *in the future* when Jesus returns and we enter "a new heaven and a new earth, the home of righteousness," (2 Peter 3:13); a place where we are told, in Revelation 7:16, "Never again will they hunger; never again will they thirst."

Matthew 6:25, 33; Proverbs 11:30a

Day Forty-Two

The LORD's love never ends; his mercies never stop. They are new every morning; LORD, your loyalty is great.

Lamentations 3:22–23 (NCV)

We know that God's ultimate goal for us is that we become more like Jesus (see Day Ten). *Because* this is a lifelong process, it seems pretty clear then that each new day offers a chance for us to be one step closer to the goal. According to the verse above, God offers us unending love and new mercies each new day. Every single day, God's mercy and love is new. God essentially wipes our slate clean every day, giving us an opportunity to start fresh and recommit ourselves to *Him* each new day.

What does that mean—to recommit ourselves to Him each new day? And how do we go about doing that? I believe the answers lie in the first four *Beatitudes*, the ones that deal specifically with our relationship with God. In these four *Beatitudes*, we are to be poor in spirit, we are to mourn, we are to be meek, and we are to hunger and thirst for righteousness.

To be *poor in spirit* is to be in poverty. To *mourn* is to be broken. To be *meek* is to be humble. To *hunger and thirst for righteousness* is to crave. All of these denote an *emptiness*. In order to grow as Christians, we must first become empty. Because when we feel poor, when we feel broken, when we feel humble, when we hunger and thirst, then we want to be filled; we want to feel better, we want to change our circumstances, and Jesus is the remedy. We must be completely emptied of ourselves so that we can be filled, instead, with Jesus. This requires *daily* maintenance. Just as God offers us new mercies each new day, so should we offer ourselves to Him anew each new day.

Psalm 98:1a; Isaiah 42:10a (MSG)

Day Forty-Three

For he satisfies the thirsty and fills the hungry with good things.

Psalm 107:9, NLT

The verse above highlights the fact that God "satisfies the thirsty and fills the hungry." Our job, therefore, *is* to hunger and thirst. We *want* to be empty, because it is in that emptiness that we can be filled with what will truly satisfy: Jesus. We don't want to just be hungry and thirsty for Jesus on Sunday mornings as we head to church. Instead, we need to hunger and thirst for Him fresh and new each day, for as we learned yesterday, His mercies for us are new each day.

In the first four *Beatitudes*, Jesus essentially calls us blessed when we are empty. Following the first four *Beatitudes* gives us a process for this daily emptying of ourselves so that we may be filled, instead, with Jesus. We simply come to God in prayer, saying:

"God, I recognize my **nothingness** compared to You, and I know that, while I am nothing compared to you, I am nothing apart from You. I need You in my life. God, I **mourn** over what separates me from You, and I'm sorry for my sins and confess them before You now. [confess your sins] And I thank You that You comfort me with

Your forgiveness. God, I come before You in **humbleness**, and I submit my life to You. God, I **hunger and thirst for righteousness**. I desire to know and follow Your will and plan for me this day. God, I come before You empty, asking that You fill me. While there will be many things in this world fighting for my devotion, I ask that You fill me by Your Holy Spirit and help me live for You. In Jesus' Name, Amen."

Matthew 5:3-6

Day Forty-Four

You have made known to me the paths of life; you will fill me with joy in your presence.

Acts 2:28

Whenever we are going to plant something, we must first prepare the soil to receive whatever is to be planted. First, the soil must be completely free from any other kind of growth within it — no plants, no weeds, and no impurities. It must be ready to receive what will be planted. It must be emptied so that it can be filled. Starting out empty will ensure that its growth will be the most fruitful.

Likewise, we must be completely emptied of *ourselves* — our self-sufficiency, our sins, our pride, and our self-guided misdirection. Then we will be ready for Jesus to fill us as He desires, making us into people who are completely dependent upon Him and willing to submit themselves to Him. When it is Jesus who fills us, our growth will be the most fruitful, as He transforms us into the images He desires — those who are more like *Him*.

Once we have been emptied of ourselves, as evidenced by the characteristics in our lives of poverty, brokenness, humility, and craving, then we are ready to be filled. As we come to Jesus each day, completely emptying ourselves before Him, He will never leave us empty. On the contrary, He will delight in filling us with Himself.

Are you ready to be filled with Jesus?

Psalm 81:10; Romans 15:13

Day Forty-Five

But then God our Savior showed us his kindness and love. He saved us, not because of the good things we did, but because of his mercy. He washed away our sins and gave us a new life through the Holy Spirit. He generously poured out the Spirit upon us because of what Jesus Christ our Savior did.

Titus 3:4–6 (NLT)

Now that we know the importance of emptying ourselves, we are ready for the filling to begin. The next four *Beatitudes* deal with our relationship with others, an area where the fruit we bear is most evident. Remember that "fruit" is evidence. If we want our lives to show evidence that we love and follow after Jesus, then we will seek Jesus each day to fill us anew, so that our lives will be the most fruitful.

As we look to the fifth *Beatitude*, we learn just what it means to be merciful. To be merciful is to be compassionate, forgiving, and generous. When we are merciful to others, we get inside their skin, seeking to see things as they see things, and to feel things as they feel them. To be shown mercy is to be treated with forgiveness and compassion, not what we *deserve*, but what we *need*.

Looking to the verse above, we are forgiven and saved not because of any good on our part, but because of God's mercy through Jesus. What did God do through Jesus? He symbolically placed all of our sins — past, present, and future — upon Jesus as He hung on the cross and died. That is because the punishment for sin is death. But then, God raised Him from the dead so that through His death and through His resurrection back to life we could be forgiven and live eternally. All done — not because we earned it or deserved it — but because God is merciful. Through Jesus, He gave us not what we deserved, but what we needed. That's mercy.

Ephesians 2:4–5 (NLT); 1 Peter 1:3

Day Forty-Six

Blessed are the merciful, for they will be shown mercy.

Matthew 5:7

In the fifth *Beatitude*, Jesus calls blessed those who are merciful. When we consider the great gift of mercy that God gave to us through the death of Jesus, how can we be anything but merciful? Through Jesus, we have forgiveness of our sins and eternal life in heaven. Through Jesus, we have not what we deserve, but what we need. Jesus tells us, in Matthew 6, that if we want to continue to receive God's mercy and forgiveness, we must show mercy to, and forgive, others.

How are we to show mercy? God's Word answers this question. We are to show mercy to others by being gentle with sinners. In Matthew 7:3, we learn that, instead of being so quick to point out the sin and wrong in others, we need to take a look at ourselves. Are we without sin? Of course not. So, we first need to repent and be sorry for our own sins before we point out any sin or wrong in another. And then, instead of judging and criticizing, we need to remember God's mercy to us, and in turn be merciful to others. Being merciful is not only forgiving others, but gently pointing out to them their sins so that they will seek God's mercy and forgiveness.

We are to show mercy to others by helping those in need of help. Galatians 6:10 tells us that we should do good to others whenever we have the chance. Being merciful to others is not judging the need of others, but reaching out and helping however we can. Being merciful is giving others not necessarily what they deserve, but what they need. When we show mercy, we will be blessed *now* with God's mercy and forgiveness, and we will be blessed *in the future* with God's ultimate mercy in our eternal home in heaven.

Matthew 6:14–15 (NLT); Matthew 7:3 (NCV);

Galatians 6:10 (NLT)

Day Forty-Seven

Blessed are the pure in heart, for they will see God.

Matthew 5:8

In the sixth *Beatitude*, Jesus calls blessed those who are pure in heart. Clean, spotless, uncorrupted, and uncontaminated come to mind when we think of the word pure. Knowing that this is how God desires for our hearts to be, what does that mean? First and foremost, it means that our hearts must be clean and without sin. In the Bible, we are shown that our hearts determine what we think, say, and do. Again, we see the importance of emptying ourselves before God and confessing our sins to Him daily. A sin-filled heart can never be pure.

Once we've been forgiven, how can we *keep* our hearts pure? Psalm 119 answers this. We keep our hearts and lives pure by obeying the Word of God. We keep our hearts and lives pure by not being double-minded. In other words, we make sure that our words match our actions. That means that we must guard against saying we love God and regularly going to church, yet going right back to a worldly mindset of putting ourselves and our flesh over and above the will of God the minute we leave church. The pure in heart not only say they love God, but their actions show it.

If we want to be *pure in heart*, we will be quick to

confess our sins and ask for forgiveness. We will keep our personal relationship with God active by staying in good communication with Him in praying and listening. We will learn His Word and do what it says. And we will put Him first in our lives and ourselves last. What is the blessing we will receive *now* when we are pure in heart? We will "*see* God." Because of our personal relationship with Him, we will be able to know Him better and, therefore, know His will and know what He would have us to do. The *future* blessing is that we will actually *see* Him, face-to-face, in our heavenly home.

Psalm 119:9 (NCV); James 4:8; 1 John 3:2–3

Day Forty-Eight

Blessed are the peacemakers, for they will be called children of God.

Matthew 5:9

In the seventh *Beatitude*, Jesus calls those who are peacemakers blessed. Peace is order, calm, agreement. In this *Beatitude*, Jesus calls us to be peace*makers*. Being a peacemaker is about those of us who have received the peace of being right with God exhibiting that peace to others. You see, when we believe that Jesus died on the cross for our sins and that God then raised Him from the dead, we are at peace with God. Jesus' death brought us that peace, according to Romans 5:1.

As we learned, if we want to receive mercy from God, then we need to show mercy to others. If we want to keep our hearts pure, then we need to obey what God tells us in His word and stay close to Him. And, if we want to be a peacemaker, we must first be at peace with God through belief in His Son, Jesus. When we are peace*makers*, we become people who seek resolution over conflict. We become people who do not strive to win at all costs, but who choose to be humble. We become people who reflect Jesus.

If we want to be the peacemakers that God calls us to be, then we need to have a disregard for the way of the world, which places importance on getting our own way. The world's attitude is to win no matter what, to have our own way no matter what. It is argumentative, antagonistic, and prideful. Peacemakers, on the other hand, follow after God's Word in James: they are "pure; then peace-loving, considerate, submissive, full of mercy and good fruit, impartial and sincere" (James 3:17).

Peacemakers "will be called sons of God." They will be blessed *now* as they become *more* like Jesus. They will be blessed *in the future* when Jesus returns and they become *just* like Him.

Romans 5:1 (NLT); James 3:17–18; 1 John 3:2 (NLT)

Day Forty-Nine

Blessed are those who are persecuted because of righteous-

ness ...

Matthew 5:10a

In the eighth, and final, *Beatitude*, Jesus calls blessed "those who are persecuted." What does it mean to be persecuted? It means to be oppressed, harassed, and tormented. Many people are persecuted every day around the world. They may be bullied, harassed, beaten up, or even murdered because of their race, their gender, their sexual orientation, or just because a bully feels entitled. But, to be "persecuted because of righteousness" is a whole other matter. To understand what Jesus means here, we first must understand what righteousness is. Psalm 119 tells us that *all* of God's commands are righteous. That means that every word *in* the Word of God is a *command* of God, meant to teach us how to live right, how to do right, and how to be in a right relationship with both God and others. To live in righteousness is to be obedient to the Word of God.

Knowing this, therefore, shows us that to be persecuted because of righteousness means to be oppressed, harassed, tormented, or bullied because of living in obedience to, or living right in the eyes of, God. One very important thing to remember is that God's biggest enemy is the *source* of persecution for righteousness: Satan, or the devil. That's just what Jesus told those who claimed to follow Him but didn't obey Him, in His words in John 8. Satan's goal is to get us off track, to get us to give up, from following after Jesus and living right. And, if he can't get us to give up completely, he tries to at least get us to compromise, to keep one foot with God and one in the world. We cannot, and should not, compromise or respond in fear, but should instead dig in our heels and go all in with God.

Psalm 119:172; John 8:42, 44, 47 (NCV)

Day Fifty

... for theirs is the kingdom of heaven.

Matthew 5:10b

When we are mistreated for following after and obeying God, how do we keep from responding in fear or compromise? It all goes back to that *personal relationship* with God (see Days Three through Eight). What will keep us from caving into fear, or even compromising in our walk with God, is a personal relationship with Him. A *daily* commitment to pray, listen, and read and learn His Word. A *daily* commitment to know Him more. First Peter 4 tells us exactly what we should do when we suffer "persecution because of righteousness," and that is to keep on doing right and trust God.

When we are persecuted for righteousness and we continue to maintain our righteousness and live in obedience to God, instead of giving in to fear or compromise, 1 Peter 4:14 tells us that the Spirit of God will come upon us and make us more like Jesus. That is our blessing *in the present*. Our *future* blessing is the promise of an eternal, heavenly home with our Creator God.

The *Beatitudes* help us see that Jesus came not only to save us so that we could live eternally in heaven at the end of our earthly lives — our *future* blessing — but so that we could live abundant, purposeful lives here on earth. He doesn't want us to stay the same, but He wants to grow us and make us more and more like Him. In fact, as we develop each of the eight *Beatitude* characteristics, we are blessed *in the present* by being made more like Jesus. God's plan and purpose for our lives will never be accomplished if we compromise and try to have one foot in the world and one with Him. Instead, His perfect plan and purpose will only be fulfilled if we decide to go all in, and live our lives in obedience to Him, just as Jesus did.

1 Peter 4:12–14, 19 (NLT)

Day Fifty-One

But blessed is the man who trusts in the LORD, whose confidence is in him. He will be like a tree planted by the water that sends out its roots by the stream. It does not fear when heat comes; its leaves are always green. It has no worries in a year of drought and never fails to bear fruit.

Jeremiah 17:7–8

Embodying the character traits outlined in the *Beatitudes* helps us develop our relationship with Jesus because it forces us to realize and acknowledge our *daily* need for Him. This is going to help us stay on the path of solid ground (see Day Three), and it would be all we would need to do if we lived in a world alone with God. But, that's not how the world is. We live in a world that is always shifting, and with people who are ever-changing, so we have to learn not only how to stay on solid ground, but how to move forward and actually walk on that solid ground.

We have spent much time discussing God's command to us in Colossians 1:10 — that we bear fruit and grow. We don't want to grow comfortable and then stand still. Instead, we want to be like the tree in the verse above from Jeremiah "that sends out its roots by the stream." We want to continue reaching out to our life-giving Source, Jesus, to take nourishment and gain knowledge. Then, like the tree above, we will never fail to bear fruit.

2 Peter 3:18; John 15:8 (NCV)

Day Fifty-Two

You are the salt of the earth.

Matthew 5:13a

After Jesus listed all of the character traits that He wants us to have, He spoke the words, from the verse above, which ties in perfectly with the *Beatitudes*. Jesus spoke these words to His followers then, and His words are the same to those of us who follow Him today. He calls us "the salt of the earth." What did Jesus mean? Looking into the different uses of salt will show us what Jesus meant:

- Salt disinfects wounds so that they can heal. This stings at first, but then the healing takes place. We are to **show mercy** to others by forgiving them when they sin against us and, in love, showing them their sin. This would sting, like salt, because no one likes to see what they've done wrong. But, in the end, like salt, it helps them heal because it leads them to God for forgiveness and a new start.

- Because of its pure and lasting quality, salt was used to seal an agreement between people in biblical times. We are to have a **pure heart**. We will show our hearts to be pure, like salt, when we don't allow the world or the people in it to distract us from our walk with Jesus.

- Salt adds taste to things. It makes them more pleasurable to eat because they have a good flavor. We are to be **peacemakers**. When we are humble and peaceful, not argumentative and proud, we make God and His Word more attractive to others and give them a good "flavor," like salt.

- In Old Testament times, salt was to be added to offerings presented to God. We are to keep following Jesus, even if others **persecute** or mistreat us for doing so. In this way we, like salt, offer *ourselves* before Him.

Luke 17:3 (NCV); Ezekiel 11:19–20; John 13:35; 1 Peter 4:16

Day Fifty-Three

But if the salt loses its salty taste, it cannot be made salty again. It is good for nothing, except to be thrown out and walked on.

Matthew 5:13b (NCV)

After Jesus calls us the "salt of the earth," He says that if salt loses its salty taste, then it is worthless, as noted in the verse above. What would make us lose our "salty taste?" A failure for us to walk our talk, a failure to live out our Christian beliefs, would cause us to lose our *saltiness*. If we don't let our actions show that we love and follow after Jesus, then it dilutes our saltiness.

If salt were to lose its saltiness, its very essence would be taken away. It would no longer sting, much less heal. It would no longer have good flavor. If the essence of salt were removed, it would no longer have its purity, making it an unworthy offering. Likewise, if we say we love and follow Jesus, yet refuse to forgive others and show them the mercy and forgiveness of Jesus, then we have lost the very essence of our saltiness. If we say we love and follow Jesus, yet allow the world or others to distract us from following Him, then we have lost the very essence of our saltiness. If we say we love and follow Jesus, yet are argumentative and prideful, then we have lost the very essence of our saltiness. And if we say we love and follow Jesus yet allow hardships to shake our trust in Him, then we have lost the very essence of our saltiness.

Salt heals, is pure and lasting, and adds flavor, and Jesus wants us to have these same traits. When we are merciful, when we have pure hearts, when we are peacemakers, then we will be full of salty flavor that we can offer before God and use to share Him with others. We can be "the salt of the earth."

Titus 2:7a; Titus 2:11–12 (NCV)

Day Fifty-Four

You are the light that gives light to the world.
Matthew 5:14a (NCV)

After calling us "the salt of the earth," Jesus then calls us "the light that gives light to the world." Again, these words tie in perfectly with the *Beatitudes*. What did Jesus mean? As with salt, if we look into the different uses of light, we will see what Jesus meant by His statement:

- Light shines to overcome the darkness and make things visible. We are to **show mercy** by being forgiving and loving toward others, even if they don't deserve it. Part of this requires that we gently show others a sin or wrong in their lives, while helping them see that forgiveness is found in God. Like light, when we show mercy, we act to make things visible [sin] and overcome the darkness by leading others to the Source of all Light—God.

- Light can be reflected. Jesus tells us, in John 8:12, "I am the light of the world. Whoever follows me will never walk in darkness, but will have the light of life." We are to have a **pure heart**. When we don't allow the world or the people around us to distract us from following after Jesus then, like light, we can truly reflect the "light of the world."

- Light is a guide. We are to be **peacemakers**. When we don't love arguing and upsetting others in order to win or try to get ahead, then we, like light, act as a guide, a good example of what it means to follow Jesus.

- Light is meant to be seen and noticed. We are to keep following Jesus, even if we are **persecuted**, or treated badly for it. That means that a Jesus-follower, like light, is to be seen and noticed. If we keep following Jesus, His light will shine through us; we just have to keep following Him.

Jude 22–23 (NLT); 2 Corinthians 7:1 (NLT);
Psalm 34:14; 1 Timothy 6:12 (NLT)

Day Fifty-Five

A city that is built on a hill cannot be hidden. And people don't hide a light under a bowl. They put it on a lampstand so the light shines for all the people in the house. In the same way, you should be a light for other people. Live so that they will see the good things you do and will praise your Father in heaven.

Matthew 5:14b–16 (NCV)

Jesus says that we are "the light that gives light to the world," and in the above verses, He says that light is meant to shine and not be hidden. He says that we are to live in such a way that the good things we do will point back to God — that *this* is letting our lights shine.

If a light were lit, then hidden under a bowl, it would defeat its very purpose. It would no longer guide or reflect. It would no longer be seen or noticed. Likewise, if we say we love and follow Jesus, yet fail to show it in our actions, then we defeat the very purpose of being a light. We hide our light when we try to follow after a world that puts "me first," or when we let our peers influence whether or not we follow after Jesus. Those actions are an attempt to hide the fact that we follow Him, thus hiding His light inside of us. In this way, we defeat the very purpose of being a light.

Light overcomes the darkness and makes things visible

—it reflects, it guides. Light is meant to be seen and noticed, and Jesus wants us to have these same traits. When we are merciful, when we have pure hearts, when we are peacemakers, then we will be filled with His light that we can offer before Him, and shine forth to share Him with others. We can be "the light that gives light to the world."

Psalm 36:9; Isaiah 2:5 (NLT); Isaiah 60:1

Day Fifty-Six

Don't copy the behavior and customs of this world, but let God transform you into a new person by changing the way you think. Then you will know what God wants you to do, and you will know how good and pleasing and perfect his will really is.

Romans 12:2 (NLT)

By now we surely know that God wants our lives to bear fruit for Him. He wants our lives to show that we love and follow Him. Knowing this, it is vitally important for us to know that every word we speak, every action we take, and every sin we commit begins in the mind — *in our thoughts*. First we think it, and then we say it or do it. Therefore, we must learn how to bear fruit in our thoughts.

When we first believe in Jesus, the Bible tells us that we are made new. We are called to be different than an unbelieving world. Before we believed, we were the same as the world; but now that we believe, we are to be new and different. This "new creation" begins with a new mind. God's Word calls us to be changed and made new in our way of thinking. Instead of thinking about what we want to say or do, or what the world thinks we should say or do, or what our friends think we should say or do, we should instead be thinking about what Jesus would have us say or do. That means that even our very thoughts need to bear fruit, or show evidence, that we follow after Jesus.

How can we possibly bear fruit in our thoughts? We can bear fruit in our thoughts by thinking on the things of God, not on earthly things. We can bear fruit in our thoughts by deliberately making our thoughts obedient to God, choosing to think on things that please Him.

James 1:14–15 (NCV); 2 Corinthians 5:17;

Colossians 3:2; 2 Corinthians 10:5

Day Fifty-Seven

Careless words stab like a sword, but wise words bring healing.

Proverbs 12:18 (NCV)

The Bible makes clear to us that we are to bear fruit not only in our thoughts, but in our words as well. Many verses emphasize the importance of *thinking* before we speak. Again, we see how vital it is for us to learn to bear fruit in our *thoughts*, first and foremost. We so often seem to think sinning is just what we say or do. But if we were to only realize how vital it is to bear fruit in our thoughts, we would see that gaining control over our thoughts actually results in sinning *less* with our words and actions.

If we want to bear fruit in our thoughts, we are going to need to work at it! Our minds are going to be naturally drawn to the things of this world, so we're going to have to decide to *set* them on heavenly things. We're going to need to fill our minds with Jesus. The same is true if we want to bear fruit in our words. It is so easy for us to conform or adapt to the world's way of speaking freely and often. Bearing fruit in our words, instead, calls for us to measure our words carefully because the more we talk, the more likely we are to sin with our words. Bearing fruit in our words calls for us to be quick to listen but slow to speak.

If we want to bear fruit in our words, it will take a deliberate effort on our part to control our tongues. If Jesus fills our *thoughts*, it will be much easier for our *words* to reflect Him.

Proverbs 10:19; 21:23 (NCV)

Ecclesiastes 5:2 (MSG); James 1:19; 3:2 (NLT)

Day Fifty-Eight

Let your conversation be always full of grace, seasoned with salt, so that you may know how to answer everyone.

Colossians 4:6

In the above verse, we see that God desires for even our very speech to be "seasoned with salt." In order to understand what He means by that, we need to look, again, to the different uses of salt:

- Salt disinfects and heals. Our speech will be *seasoned with salt* when we show mercy by speaking patiently and lovingly to others, forgiving them, and gently correcting them when they sin.

- Salt is pure and lasting. Our speech will be *seasoned with salt* when we keep our hearts pure, and refuse to allow ourselves to be influenced to gossip about or criticize others with our words.

- Salt adds taste to things and gives them flavor. Our speech will be *seasoned with salt* when we speak peacefully and are not argumentative. Our speech will be *seasoned with salt* when we consider that we are Jesus' representatives here on earth, and speak in such a way as to attract others to Him.

- Salt was used in offerings made to God. Our speech will be *seasoned with salt* when we are ready and willing to speak about God to others, without fear or shame, offering our mouths to be used by Him.

Ephesians 4:32; 2 Timothy 4:2b; Leviticus 19:16a (MSG)
Philippians 2:14; 2 Timothy 4:2a (NLT)

Day Fifty-Nine

Jesus replied, "Love the Lord your God with all your heart and with all your soul and with all your mind." This is the first and greatest commandment. And the second is like it: "Love your neighbor as yourself."

Matthew 22:37–39

We now know that Jesus wants our lives to bear fruit, but we must never be confused about why. Jesus wants our lives to bear fruit, not so that we look good, and not to show what good little Christians we are. Instead, Jesus wants our lives to bear fruit, to make *God* look good. It's to draw others to *Him*. That is what it means to truly live in obedience to the verses above. We want others to see Jesus in us so that they will be drawn to Him. We want to attract others to Jesus so that they will come to know Him as their Lord and Savior — so that they can have forgiveness of their sins and eternal life.

We have seen how to bear fruit in our thoughts and words, and now we look to how we can bear fruit in our actions. Again, we go straight to the Word of God for answers. Repeatedly, the Bible tells us that we must not merely read the Word, but do what it says. If we want our lives to bear fruit, if we want to show evidence in our lives that we love and follow after Jesus, then we have got to be people who know and obey His Word. We can't *do* His Word if we don't *know* His Word.

Second Timothy 3:16 tells us that every single word in the Bible is inspired by God and is to be used by us so that we may know how to live the life God created us to live. Once we read it and know it, it is our duty to then *do* it. Then we can be people whose actions bear fruit.

2 Timothy 3:16 (NCV); James 1:22 (NIV, MSG);

James 1:23–25 (NCV)

Day Sixty

If we are living now by the Holy Spirit, let us follow the Holy Spirit's leading in every part of our lives.

Galatians 5:25 (NLT)

On Day Twenty-Six, we learned that when we allow the Holy Spirit to control our minds, our lives begin to show evidence that He is in control. That evidence comes in the form of *fruit* that the Holy Spirit produces in us. Without the Holy Spirit's help, we would be unable to produce this fruit in our lives. The requirement is that we *live by the Holy Spirit*. As we learned, one of the jobs of the Holy Spirit is to counsel us — to teach us how to live a life that is pleasing to God (see Day Twenty-Two). When we live by the Holy Spirit, we *follow* His counsel. The ability to bear fruit in our thoughts, in our words, and in our actions comes about when we "follow the Spirit's leading in every part of our lives."

When we follow after the desires of our flesh, or sinful nature, it will lead us to do the opposite of what the Holy Spirit would lead us to do. This is why Jesus asks the Father to send His Holy Spirit to dwell within us — to help us with this struggle because, on our own, we are inclined to do wrong. The Holy Spirit will counsel us between right and wrong, and actually help us to do right. And, if that were not enough, the Holy Spirit will work in us to enable us to bear fruit. Our job is to follow His lead.

Galatians 5:19–21; Galatians 5:24–25 (NCV)

Day Sixty-One

But the fruit of the Spirit is love ...

Galatians 5:22

First John 4 tells us that the source of love is God, because God *is* love. God's very nature, or makeup, is love itself. This unique kind of love, which can only come from God Himself, is called *agape* love. This special kind of love that originates, and can only come from God, is different from love as we know it. It is not a romantic love, nor the love found between friends or brothers. Instead, it is a love that is completely self-sacrificing and unselfish.

In our human nature, it is impossible for us to embody and express this kind of sacrificial, selfless love that God has for us. However, Romans 5:5 tells us that "God has poured out his love into our hearts by the Holy Spirit, whom he has given us." This *agape* love cannot be contained in our flesh nor exhibited in our lives without the in-pouring of God's *own* love into our hearts by the gift of His Holy Spirit. When we live by the Holy Spirit, following His lead as He counsels us throughout our lives, He will enable us to bear the fruit of this sacrificial, *agape* love. He will enable us to love others sacrificially and selflessly, thus displaying clear evidence that we love and follow Him. With the Holy Spirit's help, our love can be a reflection of the love God has for us.

Through His Holy Spirit, God makes possible what is impossible for us, for nothing is impossible for Him!

1 John 4:7–12; Luke 1:37

Day Sixty-Two

I command you to love each other in the same way that I love

you.

John 15:12 (NLT)

In the above verse, we see that Jesus actually *commands* us to love as He loves us. That means that Jesus calls for us to display that sacrificial, selfless, *agape* love to others. John 15:13 (NLT) goes further to say, "And here is how to measure it—the greatest love is shown when people lay down their lives for their friends." How does Jesus love us? He showed us the greatest love anyone could show—He gave His life for us on the cross. He took the punishment that our sins deserve, though He was sinless. And He *commands* us to love others as He loves us—with sacrificial, selfless, *agape* love. And by His Holy Spirit, we are enabled to love in this way.

How do we show Jesus that we love Him? Jesus tells us the answer three times in John 14. We show Jesus that we love Him by obeying Him. We are enabled to bear fruit and love sacrificially when we obey the promptings, or counsel, of the Holy Spirit in us. As the Bible makes so clear to us, our obedience is the key to showing evidence that we love and follow after Jesus. And loving others is how we show ourselves to be the Christians that we claim to be. Our love for others is the greatest expression of our Christianity, and what truly sets us apart as children of a loving God.

John 13:34–35; John 14:15, 21, 23–24 (NLT)

Day Sixty-Three

Jesus told him, "Go and do likewise."

Luke 10:37b

We all know how easy it is for us to love those we care about. However, in Matthew 5, Jesus tells us to also love our enemies. Why would Jesus do this? Again, we are told in His Word to love "in the same way" as He loves us. Did Jesus not bear *every* sin and *every* wrong from *every* human upon Him as He died on the cross? Even though we should be considered His enemies because of our sins, He still loves us, even dying for us. Sacrificial love enables us to love even our enemies as ourselves.

Nowhere is this illustrated more clearly than in the story of the Good Samaritan, told by Jesus in Luke 10. In this story, a Jewish man was attacked by bandits. He was beaten and robbed and left for dead on the side of the road. When a Jewish priest came along and saw the man, he crossed to the other side of the road and did nothing. Then a Levite, or religious leader, who was walking by also saw the man. He, too, crossed by on the other side, ignoring the dying man. Following that, a Samaritan came along. The Samaritans were the enemies of the Jews. As the Samaritan came closer to the dying man, he had compassion on him. He stopped and treated his wounds. He then put him on his donkey and took him to an inn and paid for them to take care of him. After telling the story, Jesus then said, "Go and do likewise."

When we live by the Holy Spirit and follow His counsel throughout our lives, He will work in us and through us, enabling us to bear fruit, and display that same sacrificial, selfless, *agape* love that God Himself has for us. With this sacrificial love, we are enabled to truly love our neighbors—or *all* people—as ourselves. "But the fruit of the Spirit is love" (Galatians 5:22).

Matthew 5:43–48 (NCV); Luke 10:25–37

Day Sixty-Four

But the fruit of the Spirit is love, joy ...
Galatians 5:22

The next component of the "fruit of the Spirit" is joy. Many will say that joy is the same as happiness. However, happiness is based on outer things, things that will grow old or fade away. When you get something new, it makes you happy. But, after a time, you lose interest in it or forget about it, or maybe it even breaks. Then the happiness you initially felt for it goes away. However, there is a feeling of happiness or gladness that goes much deeper and lasts forever, a feeling of gladness that is on the *inside* — one that is not based on outer things. That kind of inner gladness is called joy.

The difference between happiness and joy is that happiness is based on what happens to us; it's based on our circumstances. If everything is right, then we can be happy. But the moment something goes wrong or our circumstances change, that happiness is gone. Joy, however, goes much deeper.

Just as God is the source of love, *Jesus* is the source of joy. When the angel appeared to the shepherds, announcing the birth of Jesus, he said, "Do not be afraid. I am bringing you good news that will be a great joy to all the people. Today your Savior was born in the town of David. He is Christ, the

Lord" (Luke 2:10–11, NCV). Jesus' salvation plan is the "great joy" the angel spoke of. When we ask Jesus to come and live in our hearts, accepting His plan for salvation, then that means that we have the inner gladness that joy *is* living and dwelling *within us*. Inviting Jesus into our hearts literally fills our hearts with joy. And with the Holy Spirit's help, our joy can lead others to Jesus.

Psalm 16:9 (NLT); 1 Peter 1:8 (NCV)

Day Sixty-Five

When you obey me, you remain in my love, just as I obey my Father and remain in his love. I have told you this so that you will be filled with my joy. Yes, your joy will overflow!

John 15:10–11 (NLT)

We learned that Jesus commands us to love each other as He loves us — with sacrificial, selfless, *agape* love. Before He gave us that command, in John 15:12, He spoke the words in the verses above. Once again, we see that our obedience to Jesus is the key: it keeps us close to Him, helping us to remain in His love. When we are obedient to Him, and remain in His love, He tells us that we will be filled with His joy.

Since Jesus is the source of joy then, if He lives in our hearts, does that mean that we will never be sad or down? Of course not. But, joy is what allows us to be able to lift up our heads, no matter what troubles we face. When we have joy in our hearts, we know that it is Jesus who will truly fulfill us and comfort us.

Unlike happiness, there is a way to keep joy. Jesus tells us how in those verses from John 15, and the letters in "joy" help us remember:

J — Jesus. We must put Jesus first. He must live in our hearts, we must invite Him in, and then we must obey Him. "Remain in my love," Jesus said.

O—Others. We must put others second. "Love each other in the same way that I love you," Jesus said.

Y—You. We must put ourselves last. We must take our focus off of our circumstances and look to Jesus for fulfillment. "I have told you this so that you will be filled with my joy," Jesus said. "Yes, your joy will overflow!"

2 Corinthians 4:18 (NLT); Psalm 4:7a; 119:11–12

Day Sixty-Six

Each time he said, "My gracious favor is all you need. My power works best in your weakness."

2 Corinthians 12:9a (NLT)

We all know how easy it is to be joyful when everything seems to be going well in our lives. However, God's Word tells us in James 1 to let our *problems* be opportunities for us to have joy. How can our problems be a time for joy? Why would God want us to be joyful when we're going through hard times? James 1 tells us that our problems test our faith and give us strength and patience — *endurance* — to keep going in tough times.

The life of the Apostle Paul is such a good illustration to us of one who remained joyful in hard times. God sent Paul to minister to the Gentiles and tell them of the saving grace of Jesus (see Acts 9:15). Throughout his ministry, he was beaten, stoned, and shipwrecked. He was often hungry, thirsty, cold, and naked. He was in constant danger. And then Paul describes a nagging affliction: "a thorn in my flesh, a messenger of Satan, to torment me" (2 Corinthians 12:7, NIV). Although the Bible does not specify what this "thorn" was, we know that it caused Paul great torment. He begged for God to take it away, but God responded that His power worked best in Paul's weakness.

Although Paul did not want this "thorn" in his flesh, and although Paul prayed three times for God to take it away, he came to realize that this affliction that tormented and weakened him provided an opportunity for him to experience God's strength and power. This, then, enabled him to say, "That is why, for Christ's sake, I delight in weaknesses, in insults, in hardships, in persecutions, in difficulties. For when I am weak, then I am strong" (2 Corinthians 12:10). The Holy Spirit enabled Paul's many hardships to become opportunities for joy, opportunities in which he could *delight*.

James 1:2–4 (NLT); 2 Corinthians 11:25–27; 12:7-10

Day Sixty-Seven

For the kingdom of God is not a matter of eating and drinking, but of righteousness, peace and joy in the Holy Spirit, because anyone who serves Christ in this way is pleasing to God and approved by men."

Romans 14:17–18

As we learned yesterday, God's Word tells us to let our problems be opportunities to be joyful. We learned that our problems help us to develop endurance. What are we to do with that endurance? Hebrews 12 tells us: We are to "run with endurance the race that God has set before us" (Hebrews 12:1, NLT). We are to keep going, despite our hardships, staying on the path God has marked out for our lives. How do we do this? Hebrews 12 continues, "We do this by keeping our eyes on Jesus …" (Hebrews 12:2, NLT).

We look to Jesus — our perfect Example — to see how to let hardships become opportunities for joy. We *delight* in our weaknesses, knowing that they provide opportunities for God's power to strengthen us. And, with God's help, when we persevere through hard times and refuse to let them rob us of our inner joy, our Christian character really shines through. We become people who are pleasing to God and approved by men.

Through the Holy Spirit, God worked His power in

Paul's life, testing his faith, growing his endurance, and enabling him to remain joyful in his many hardships. Paul's joy in hardship led many to the saving grace and knowledge of Jesus. When we live by the Holy Spirit and follow His counsel, God will work His power in us, enabling us to bear fruit and display joy in our lives. Our joy — in good times and bad — can be a shining example that can lead others to the source of all joy — Jesus. "But the fruit of the Spirit is ... joy" (Galatians 5:22).

Hebrews 12:1b–3 (NLT); Psalm 28:7 (NLT)

Day Sixty-Eight

But the fruit of the Spirit is love, joy, peace ...

Galatians 5:22

The next component of the "fruit of the Spirit" is peace. Peace is an absence of war; it is a sense of harmony, calmness, and tranquility. Philippians 4 speaks of "the peace of God," a feeling of peace so great that we cannot even comprehend it. We are told to lay all our problems and worries before God in prayer, and in their place we will receive *His* peace. Peace that we have from the world comes about only when everything is right with us, and we are experiencing no trouble or hardship. "The peace of God," however, enables us to feel this harmony, calmness, and tranquility when our circumstances, and everything that is happening around us, say that we should feel the exact opposite.

Just like *agape* love and inner joy, this component of the "fruit of the Spirit" is supernatural. It could only come from God. To lay all our worries and concerns before Him, and in their place, receive His peace — a peace that goes way beyond our understanding ... *that* could only come from God through His Holy Spirit! When we trust God and live in obedience to His Word, we are blessed to receive this supernatural peace — "the peace of God" — in our lives. And when we live by the Holy Spirit, following His lead as He counsels us throughout our lives, He will enable us to bear the fruit of His supernatural peace.

Philippians 4:6–7; John 14:27 (NLT)

Day Sixty-Nine

If your sinful nature controls your mind, there is death. But if the Holy Spirit controls your mind, there is life and peace.

Romans 8:6 (NLT)

Oh, how easy it is for us to feel at peace when everything seems to be going well in our lives! But how can we experience peace when we are going through hard times and trials? On our own, apart from the Holy Spirit, it would be impossible. God's Word outlines what we need to do to experience that supernatural peace — *God's peace* — that is a gift from His Holy Spirit: "Don't worry about anything; instead, pray about everything. Tell God what you need, and thank him for all he has done" (Philippians 4:6, NLT).

Genesis describes the life of Noah, "a righteous man, blameless among the people of his time," and one who "walked with God" (Genesis 6:9). During Noah's time, God was very displeased with how the whole earth was full of corruption and decided that He was going to destroy the earth and all of its corrupt people. Noah, however, had "found favor in the eyes of the LORD" (Genesis 6:8), and God planned to spare him and his family. He told Noah to build an ark, following His exact specifications. He then told Noah to gather not only his family, but two of every living creature, and come aboard the ark to be spared as He flooded the earth.

What was Noah's response? Verse 22 tells us, "Noah did everything just as God commanded him." Rain began to fall and continued on for forty days and nights. The earth was completely flooded. All around the ark of Noah was chaos. Noah's unwavering trust and complete obedience to God, however, allowed Noah to experience *God's peace* in what was, quite literally, the storm of his life.

Trusting in God and following the counsel of His Holy Spirit in our lives allows us to experience "God's peace, which is far more wonderful than the human mind can understand,"Philippians 4:7 (NLT).

Philippians 4:6–7 (NLT); Genesis 6:5–22; Genesis 7:12, 21–24

Day Seventy

Peacemakers who sow in peace raise a harvest of
righteousness.

James 3:18

As we learned yesterday, trusting in God is essential to experiencing *His* peace. Will we trust that we can lay all our worries and fears before Him and, in exchange, receive His perfect peace? Will we believe the promises He makes to us in His Word? We live in a troubling, chaotic world, and Jesus confirms to us in John 16:33 that we *will* have trouble in this world. But He promises that *in Him* we can have peace because He has overcome the world. What that means is that, when troubles are all around us and chaos is reigning, we can turn to Jesus and He will give us peace. The world tells us, "Look around you — there is much to be troubled by, much to be afraid of." But Jesus says, "… in me you may have peace" (John 16:33).

We look to Jesus — our Prince of Peace — to provide us with a peace the world could never give us. Instead of drowning in the troubles that the storms of life heap upon us, we rest in the safety of His everlasting arms as we trust in Him. As we rest in His peace, we begin to reflect that peace to others. As we react in peace to the troubles that surround us, we become "Peacemakers who sow in peace," and who "raise a harvest of righteousness" (James 3:18).

Noah continued to trust in God and do everything "just as God commanded him" (Genesis 6:22). As he trusted and obeyed God, the Holy Spirit enabled Noah to experience peace, though the storm raged all around him. When we trust in God and His Word and live in obedience to the counsel He gives us through His Holy Spirit, He will enable us to bear fruit and display peace in our lives. That peace can be a shining reflection of the Prince of Peace and raise "a harvest of righteousness," as we lead others to Him. "But the fruit of the Spirit is … peace" (Galatians 5:22).

John 16:33; Isaiah 9:6; Deuteronomy 33:27a; Isaiah 26:3–4

Day Seventy-One

But the fruit of the Spirit is love, joy, peace, patience ...

Galatians 5:22

The next component of the fruit of the Spirit is patience. Patience is enduring in hard circumstances. Being patient means persevering, or continuing, with a positive attitude despite being delayed or provoked. Having patience means that we continue to act in a positive manner instead of reacting in anger or annoyance. The world we live in is a "me first!" world. In other words, we live in an impatient world that encourages us to do whatever it takes to put ourselves first and make things as easy as we can for ourselves. We're busy people, we don't have time to wait, and no one should expect us to wait, or at least to wait *patiently*. God's Word, however, calls us to let our patience "show itself perfectly" (James 1:4, NCV) in what we do.

As we have learned, the world's view greatly differs from God's view. As Christians, we are called to be different from the world around us. We need to always keep in mind God's ultimate goal for us: that we become more like Jesus. We need to look at our life experiences as working to achieve that goal in us. In this life, we will have troubles, we will go through trials and hard circumstances that will try and test our faith. And in all of these trials and hard circumstances, as we keep our eyes on Jesus and keep trusting in Him, the Holy Spirit will step in and produce in us the fruit of patience, enabling us to act calmly and positively when we are provoked or faced with delays. With the Holy Spirit's help, our patience will indeed "show itself perfectly" in all that we do.

James 1:4 (NCV); Romans 12:2 (NCV);
2 Corinthians 3:18 (NCV)

Day Seventy-Two

... be patient, bearing with one another in love.

Ephesians 4:2b

It is such a struggle, in today's world, to be patient people. In our fast-paced society, this attribute is not considered very realistic or even important. But God calls us in His Word to be patient. Once more, we see that, apart from the Holy Spirit working in us, this would be impossible. Our flesh wants us to react in selfishness and rage when we are faced with delays or when we are provoked or irritated. However, when we follow the lead of the Holy Spirit, then He will enable us to be people who act calmly and positively in the face of delay or irritation. He will enable us to trust in God and wait for *His* lead, instead of making our own way by reacting with *im*patience.

James reminds us of what great examples we have of "patience in the face of suffering" (James 5:10), both in the lives of the prophets and in the life of Job. The prophets were called on by God to do very dangerous, difficult tasks. Yet, throughout the Old Testament, we see the examples they left us of those who patiently endured hardships and lived their lives in trusting obedience. And, with Job, we see how he patiently endured one hardship after another. We are told, "In all this, Job did not sin by charging God with wrongdoing," even saying, "Shall we accept good from God, and not trouble?" (Job 1:22; 2:10).

God displays His great patience with us, not wanting "anyone to be lost," but wanting "all people to change their hearts and lives" (2 Peter 3:9b, NCV). And He calls us to be patient with others. As we trust in God and His Word and live by His Holy Spirit, He will enable us to bear the fruit of patience in our lives. As we respond to others with patience and bear with them in love, we reflect Jesus and help draw others to Him. "But the fruit of the Spirit is … patience" (Galatians 5:22).

James 5:10–12; Job 1:22, 2:10b; 2 Peter 3:9b (NCV); Colossians 1:11 (NCV)

Day Seventy-Three

But the fruit of the Spirit is love, joy, peace, patience,

kindness ...

Galatians 5:22

The next component of the fruit of the Spirit is kindness. To show kindness is to be friendly, generous, and considerate to others, even when we do not think they deserve it. God's Word shares the true definition of kindness in Titus 3:

> But then God our Savior showed us his kindness
> and love. He saved us, not because of the good
> things we did, but because of his mercy. He
> washed away our sins and gave us a new life
> through the Holy Spirit. He generously poured
> out the Spirit upon us because of what Jesus
> Christ our Savior did. He declared us not guilty
> because of his great kindness. And now we
> know that we will inherit eternal life. (Titus 3:4–
> 7, NLT)

Because of the Lord's great kindness, He sent His perfect Son, Jesus, to this earth to bear our punishment on the cross. Because of the Lord's great kindness, He not only forgave us, but transformed us into a new creation through His Holy Spirit. Because of the Lord's great kindness, we have been given eternal life. We have these precious gifts from God, not because we deserved them; in fact, Isaiah 64:6 tells us that "all our righteous acts are like filthy rags." Instead, we have these precious gifts because of God's mercy, because of His great kindness.

God displayed for us the ultimate act of kindness, and He calls us to be "kind and compassionate to one another," (Ephesians 4:32). He calls us to imitate Him. This means that we are to show kindness to others, whether or not we feel they deserve it. When we live in obedience to the Holy Spirit, He will enable us to bear the fruit of kindness, to be friendly, generous, and considerate to others — deserving or not. With the Holy Spirit working in us, our kindness can be a reflection of the kindness God shows to us.

Ephesians 4:32–5:2; 2 Timothy 2:24

Day Seventy-Four

So, chosen by God for this new life of love, dress in the wardrobe God picked out for you: compassion, kindness, humility, quiet strength, discipline.

Colossians 3:12 (MSG)

As God makes so clear to us in His Word, our salvation is supposed to change us. Our salvation is supposed to show evidence of a new life, and God sends His Holy Spirit to us to *enable* us to live that changed life. God sends His Holy Spirit to us to enable us to bear fruit, or show evidence that we love and follow after Jesus and are living by His Spirit. Before we believed in Jesus, and before He sent the Holy Spirit to live in us, we were led solely by our flesh, living only to please ourselves. But, now that we believe, now that we have received Jesus into our hearts, we show our love and faithfulness to Him by allowing *His Holy Spirit* to lead us. We now live to please *Him*. The result of this is a changed life, a "new life of love."

Because we are now living by the Spirit, God calls us to display kindness as if it were the very clothes we wear! This means that being friendly, generous, compassionate, and caring toward others is not just about something we do, but it is about who we are. The world around us influences us to be kind only to those who are kind to us. God's Word, however, tells us to show kindness to everyone. As we learned yesterday, it is because of the Lord's great kindness that we *have* this new life through His Spirit. And it is through the Spirit that we are enabled to bear the fruit of kindness — not just to those who are kind to us, but to *everyone*.

Romans 2:4 tells us that God's kindness leads us to repent, or turn away from, our sins. The kindness God shows us draws us to Him. With the Holy Spirit's help, we can "be kind to everyone," (2 Timothy 2:24a, NLT), imitating our kind and loving Lord and leading others to Him. "But the fruit of the Spirit is … kindness" (Galatians 5:22).

2 Timothy 2:24a (NLT); Luke 6:35–36 (MSG)

Day Seventy-Five

But the fruit of the Spirit is love, joy, peace, patience,

kindness, goodness ...

Galatians 5:22

The next component of the fruit of the Spirit is goodness. When we think of goodness, we think of that which is good, moral, and of excellent quality. God's Word tells us that, before we believed in Jesus and were filled with His Holy Spirit, we were darkness. Our unbelief caused us to live in the darkness of our sins as we followed after the desires of our flesh. But now, as believers we are "light in the Lord," says Ephesians 5:8. It goes on to say in verse 9 that the fruit, or evidence, of living as light is made up of all "goodness, righteousness and truth." What this means is that, as believers, our lives should reflect that we love and follow after Jesus; our lives should reflect *His* light. His light reflects that which is good, right, and true.

God spells out to us what is good in His eyes: "to do what is right, to love mercy, and to walk humbly with your God." (Micah 6:8, NLT). True goodness is doing what is right, according to God's Word and will. True goodness is not only having compassion for others, but actually *loving* to show that compassion by being merciful to others. True goodness is following humbly after God, and seeking to live in obedience to Him. Goodness is not just about doing good deeds. Goodness, instead, is all in how we speak to others and how we treat them. Goodness consists of living our lives in obedience to what is known as The Golden Rule: "Do for others what you would like them to do for you" (Matthew 7:12, NLT).

When we live by the Holy Spirit, following His lead as He counsels us throughout our lives, He will enable us to bear the fruit of goodness. His counsel will enable us "to do what is right, to love mercy, and to walk humbly" with our God.

Ephesians 5:8–10; Micah 6:8 (NLT); Matthew 7:12 (NLT)

Day Seventy-Six

God is the One who gives seed to the farmer and bread for food. He will give you all the seed you need and make it grow so there will be a great harvest from your goodness.

2 Corinthians 9:10 (NCV)

Consistently bearing the fruit of goodness in our lives can be very challenging in the world we live in today. There are many messages that convey to us that we should do what makes us happy, no matter what. Messages like, "if it feels good, do it," and "everyone does it." But as Christians, our standards should not be measured against the standards of the world and what everyone else is doing. Our standards are to be measured against how our guidebook, the Bible, tells us we are to live. God's Word calls us to "do good to all people" (Galatians 6:10).

Like all the other components of the fruit of the Spirit, the fruit of goodness will not come naturally to us. Displaying the fruit of goodness requires us to keep our eyes on God, and "find out what pleases" *Him* (Ephesians 5:10). The world around us influences us to do what pleases *ourselves*. We will face much pressure to conform to those self-seeking views as we seek to display goodness in our lives, but we have God's Word as a promise: He will not only supply us with the "seed," or fruit, we need, but He will make it grow.

As the Holy Spirit begins to bear the fruit of goodness in our lives, we become people who do what is right, who love mercy, and who walk humbly with our God, and others will take notice. As we follow the counsel of the Holy Spirit and strive to do what pleases the Lord, God will cause our goodness to grow in such a way that others are drawn to Him through our goodness. "But the fruit of the Spirit is ... goodness" (Galatians 5:22).

2 Corinthians 9:8; Galatians 6:10; Ephesians 2:10; Titus 2:13–14

Day Seventy-Seven

But the fruit of the Spirit is love, joy, peace, patience, kindness, goodness, faithfulness ...

Galatians 5:22

The next component of the fruit of the Spirit is faithfulness. Faithfulness is showing devotion, loyalty, and trustworthiness. Faithfulness means keeping our promises and being dependable and dedicated. God's Word says this about faithfulness in Proverbs 3:3: "Let love and faithfulness never leave you; bind them around your neck, write them on the tablet of your heart." God wants the quality of faithfulness to be so much a part of us that it is bound around our necks (for others to see), and written on our hearts (deeply ingrained into our very beings).

As Christians, all of our beliefs are based completely upon faith. Hebrews tells us that faith is "the confident assurance that what we hope for is going to happen. It is the evidence of things we cannot yet see" (Hebrews 11:1, NLT). It goes on to say, in verse 6, "So, you see, it is impossible to please God without faith. Anyone who wants to come to him must believe that there is a God and that he rewards those who sincerely seek him." Faith is trusting in something, even when we do not see it. Christianity calls for us to continually have faith, to continually trust in what we do not see — God,

Jesus, the Holy Spirit, heaven, eternal life, and all the Bible's promises yet to be fulfilled. And faithfulness is all about staying true and devoted, and trusting in God, His Word, and His promises.

As we listen to the still, small voice of the Holy Spirit as He directs us day by day, keeping us on the path God has marked out for us, He will work in us, enabling us to become people who are devoted and loyal to God, full of integrity and trustworthiness. He will enable us to bear the fruit of faithfulness.

Romans 1:17; 4:16a (NLT); Joshua 24:14a

Day Seventy-Eight

We are surrounded by a great cloud of people whose lives tell us what faith means. So let us run the race that is before us and never give up. We should remove from our lives anything that would get in the way and the sin that so easily holds us back.

Hebrews 12:1 (NCV)

In the book of Hebrews, the Bible gives us great examples of those who were filled with faithfulness. This is the "great cloud of people" spoken of in the above verse. On Day Sixty-Nine, we learned about Noah and the peace of God that he experienced during the flood. It was Noah's unwavering trust and complete obedience to God that allowed him to experience that peace. Hebrews 11 describes how Noah stayed true to God — he stayed faithful and obedient, trusting God in something that had never before happened.

Hebrews 11 describes the faithfulness of Moses, beginning with his parents. We are told that they were filled with faithfulness and trust in God. At a time when all Israelite males were put to death at birth (by order of the king), Moses' parents hid him. When they could hide him no longer, his mother made a waterproof basket for him and put him in the river. He was found by the king's daughter, who raised him as her own. As Moses grew into a man, his faithfulness set him apart. Instead of enjoying the benefits of being raised in royalty, verse 26 tells us that Moses "thought it was better to suffer for the sake of the Messiah than to own the treasures of Egypt, for he was looking ahead to the great reward that God would give him." God used him to free His chosen people, the Israelites, from their slavery in Egypt and chose him to be their leader.

God left us these examples in His Word to show us the kind of faithfulness He requires. By the Holy Spirit, we can show this same faithfulness.

Hebrews 11:7, 23–29 (NLT)

Day Seventy-Nine

A faithful man will be richly blessed ...

Proverbs 28:20a

God's Word tells us that our faithfulness will cause us to be richly blessed. Our faith and trust in God leads us to obey Him and His Word, and to follow the counsel of His Holy Spirit. That is what faithfulness is all about — trust and obedience. Our faithfulness, in turn, results in rich blessing. As we saw with the example of Noah, God richly blessed him for his faithfulness by sparing his life, as well as the lives of his family. Even more, it was because of the faithfulness of Noah that we exist today, for God would have destroyed the entire earth were it not for the faithfulness of this one man! Moses' parents were richly blessed for their faithfulness by the sparing of their son's life. God richly blessed Moses for his faithfulness — not only by sparing his life, but also by using him to save the Israelite people from the Egyptians.

God richly blessed these people for their faithfulness by using them to serve as our examples. In them, we truly see the kind of faithfulness God expects from us. The message we receive from the world is "you only live once!" The world urges us to focus on ourselves and try to get the very most we can out of this earthly life, with not a single thought to the future and the hope of a life spent in eternity. God, however, is looking for people who stay true to Him and seek *His* will in life. God is looking for the appropriate response to our faith and trust in Him: our obedience.

As we respond to God in obedience, His Holy Spirit fills us with the fruit of faithfulness. As we display the fruit of faithfulness in our lives, we will be richly blessed as God uses that faithfulness to draw others to Him. "But the fruit of the Spirit is … faithfulness" (Galatians 5:22).

Hebrews 11:39–40 (NLT); Proverbs 3:3–4

Day Eighty

But the fruit of the Spirit is love, joy, peace, patience,
kindness, goodness, faithfulness, gentleness ...

Galatians 5:22–23

The next component of the fruit of the Spirit is gentleness. Gentleness is being mild and tender, gracious and kind. Gentleness means having a controlled strength, and being even-tempered. A gentle person is a humble person. God's Word says this about gentleness: "Are there those among you who are truly wise and understanding? Then they should show it by living right and doing good things with a gentleness that comes from wisdom" (James 3:13, NCV).

As we can see from that verse, God considers it a mark of wisdom to do things with gentleness. When we not only live right and do good things, but do them with gentleness, then we show wisdom. Being wise is all about living and acting well. According to this verse, true wisdom is shown by the gentleness that we display in our spirits and in our behavior. Being calm and mild allows us to be better listeners, and better speakers, as well. The book of Proverbs makes several references to gentleness and the benefits of gentle words, making so clear to us the value God places on gentleness.

As we live by following the Holy Spirit in our lives, He

will work in us, enabling us to become people who are humble and mild, who are even-tempered and have a controlled strength. With the Holy Spirit at work in us, we can bear the fruit of gentleness in our lives.

James 3:13 (NCV); Proverbs 15:1, 4; 25:15 (NCV)

Day Eighty-One

Accept my teachings and learn from me, because I am gentle and humble in spirit, and you will find rest for your lives.
Matthew 11:29 (NCV)

It is so important that we never lose sight of God's goal for us on this earth: that we become more like His Son, Jesus. As we stay close to God and live our lives in obedience to Him and the counsel He gives us through His Holy Spirit, the Holy Spirit begins to transform us. The Holy Spirit does a work in us and through us that we are incapable of apart from Him: He causes our lives to bear fruit, or show evidence that we love and follow after Jesus. This fruit-bearing work in our lives not only shows that we love and follow after Jesus, it also reflects Jesus. The fruit that the Holy Spirit produces in us makes us more like Jesus.

As we seek to become more like Jesus, we look to the example He set for us in His Word. Jesus, Powerful Jesus, describes Himself as "gentle and humble in spirit." The One and only Perfect Son of God, who never sinned, tells us in His Word that He is gentle. He instructs us to learn from Him *because* He is "gentle and humble in spirit." Jesus' gentleness allowed Him to feel compassion for all people, which resulted in His great outpouring of mercy. Jesus' gentleness allowed Him to remain humble — His goal always being to bring glory and honor to the Father, instead of Himself.

The world we live in urges us to assert ourselves to the point of aggression to make sure we get what we want from life. But God calls us to be "completely humble and gentle"(Ephesians 4:2), to pursue gentleness (1 Timothy 6:11), and to follow the example of His Son, who is "gentle and humble in spirit." Let us be obedient to the Holy Spirit that He may make us more like Jesus.

Ephesians 4:2; 1 Timothy 6:11; 1 Peter 2:21 (NCV)

Day Eighty-Two

You should be known for the beauty that comes from within, the unfading beauty of a gentle and quiet spirit, which is so precious to God.

1 Peter 3:4 (NLT)

The Holy Spirit works in us to *produce* the fruit of the Spirit, so that we may become more like Jesus. The Holy Spirit works in us to *bear* the fruit of the Spirit, so that we can draw others to Jesus. Our duty as Christians is to reflect Jesus for the purpose of attracting others to Him. The Holy Spirit works in us, allowing us to meet this duty, for we could not do so apart from Him.

Gentleness is not a quality that is viewed of any value in the world we live in today. The world views gentleness as being a doormat, as a way of letting people walk all over you. The world views gentleness as a way of being used or taken advantage of. But God sees gentleness as something precious. As we begin to not only listen to the counsel of the Holy Spirit (that still, small voice speaking to us and leading us, helping us to know right from wrong) but also begin to obey His voice, then He begins to produce His fruit of gentleness in us.

A remarkable thing begins to happen as we follow the Holy Spirit's lead: we begin to put ourselves in another's shoes, and we begin to see others more through the eyes of

Jesus and less through our own fleshly, worldly ones. As we see others more through the eyes of Jesus, who is "gentle and humble in spirit," we embody what God calls precious (Matthew 11:29). We *reflect* Jesus to a world desperate for a good example, and we *attract* others to the only Perfect One. "But the fruit of the Spirit is ... gentleness" (Galatians 5:22–23).

Philippians 4:5; 1 Peter 3:3–4 (NCV)

Day Eighty-Three

But the fruit of the Spirit is love, joy, peace, patience,
kindness, goodness, faithfulness, gentleness and self-control.
Against such things there is no law.

Galatians 5:22–23

The last component of the fruit of the Spirit is self-control. When we think of self-control, we think of self-discipline, of being able to restrain our natural, fleshly impulses. Self-control is all about resisting what our flesh desires and, instead, choosing to do God's will in our lives. God's Word says this, "So think clearly and exercise self-control. Look forward to the special blessings that will come to you at the return of Jesus Christ." (1 Peter 1:13, NLT).

As we learned from Galatians 5:17 on Day Twenty-One, we will always battle between choosing what our flesh (the sinful part of us) desires and what the Holy Spirit desires. God's Word tells us that we will never be free from this conflict. We will be faced numerous times every day with having to choose what our flesh desires or what the Holy Spirit desires. We can be sure of this: When we follow after the desires of our flesh, our flesh will always lead us to do the opposite of what the Holy Spirit would lead us to do. Self-control is all about mastering these desires of our flesh, the root of our sin and a problem since Adam and Eve. God tells us in His Word that sin desires to have us, but we must master it.

God is so gracious and kind to us that not only does He tell us the importance of having self-control, but He also provides us with His Holy Spirit to develop that self-control in us. As we live by following the counsel of the Holy Spirit, He will work in us, enabling us to restrain and resist our fleshly impulses and choose to follow the will of God. With the Holy Spirit at work in us, we can bear the fruit of self-control in our lives.

1 Peter 1:13 (NLT); Galatians 5:17; Genesis 4:7

Day Eighty-Four

For the grace of God that brings salvation has appeared to all men. It teaches us to say 'No' to ungodliness and worldly passions, and to live self-controlled, upright and godly lives in this present age ...

Titus 2:11–12

In the above verse, we are told that God's grace has given us the gift of salvation. Because God has given us favor that we do not deserve (grace), we have the gift of forgiveness and eternal life. God's grace has also taught us in His Word that we are to resist the desires of our flesh and the temptations from the world around us. God's grace has given us the gift of His Holy Spirit to help us live the "self-controlled, upright and godly lives" that He has commanded us to live.

Every sin that we commit comes from when we have put ourselves before God, and where we have failed to exercise self-control. Our flesh wants what it wants, when it wants it! The world we live in today continually urges us to focus solely on ourselves and getting what we want out of life. We are constantly bombarded with messages that *things* will make us happy, and we should do all we can to acquire those *things*. The world urges us to be self-centered, rather than self-controlled. But God tells us, in 1 Peter 1:13, to "prepare" our minds "for action," and to be "self-controlled." By this we know that God wants us to not only expect for these temptations to come, but to "prepare" for them by being "self-controlled."

In our own flesh and by our own strength, we can never have the self-control needed to resist all the desires of our flesh and the temptations from the world around us. May we be ever thankful to God that the Holy Spirit inside of us is "greater than the devil, who is in the world" (1 John 4:4, NCV). By the Holy Spirit, we can say "No" to these desires and temptations. By the Holy Spirit, we can be "self-controlled."

1 Thessalonians 5:6; 1 Peter 5:8; 1 John 4:4 (NCV)

Day Eighty-Five

So make every effort to apply the benefits of these promises to your life. Then your faith will produce a life of moral excellence. A life of moral excellence leads to knowing God better. Knowing God better leads to self-control. Self-control leads to patient endurance, and patient endurance leads to godliness. Godliness leads to love for other Christians, and finally you will grow to have genuine love for everyone. The more you grow like this, the more you will become productive and useful in your knowledge of our Lord Jesus Christ.

2 Peter 1:5–8 (NLT)

From the above verse, we see that knowing God has a direct correlation to developing self-control. The more we know God, the more we trust Him, the more we honor Him, and the more we obey Him. The more we know God, the more we want His will over our own — the more we have self-control. Having self-control leads us to be more godly, making us more like Jesus.

Self-control is a quality that is sorely lacking in our world today. The many technological advances and discoveries have led us to expect instant gratification. We are so used to having what we want at our fingertips, in an instant, that it has greatly inhibited our ability to do without, or not to demand our own way. Here we see that *knowing God* is essential. When we *really* know Him — when we live our lives praying and seeking His will, and reading and learning His Word, our love for Him will fill us with a desire to want what *He* wants for our lives. This will lead us to follow the counsel He gives us through His Holy Spirit.

As the Holy Spirit works in us, developing the fruit of self-control and making us more like Jesus, we are filled with a genuine "love for everyone." Our obedience to the Holy Spirit and our love for others makes us "productive and useful" to God, and our lives become shining examples that draw others to Him. "But the fruit of the Spirit is … self-control" (Galatians 5:22–23).

Proverbs 25:28; 1 Corinthians 9:24–27 (NLT)

Day Eighty-Six

Do not hold back the work of the Holy Spirit.

1 Thessalonians 5:19 (NCV)

We are told in John 15 that Jesus is the vine and we are the branches. As we learned on Day Twenty-Seven, we need to "remain in" Jesus in order to stay connected to that vine. We need to maintain our relationship with Him by praying and listening to Him, and by reading and studying God's Word. This keeps us connected to Jesus, the Vine. John also tells us that God is the gardener. "He cuts off every branch that doesn't produce fruit, and he prunes the branches that do bear fruit so they will produce even more" (John 15:2, NLT).

God accomplishes this fruit-bearing through His Holy Spirit. Our lives will only bear the fruit of the Spirit when we give Him control. We must be obedient to the counsel God gives us through His Holy Spirit. We "hold back the work of the Holy Spirit" when we ignore His leading and follow our own sinful desires. The result of this is a life that fails to bear fruit and is of no use to God, for God created us to bear fruit. God created us to display evidence that we love and follow after Him.

As our lives begin to bear the fruit of the Spirit, displaying such godly qualities that could only come from God Himself, *He* gets the glory and honor. Rather than drawing attention to ourselves, the fruit the Holy Spirit produces in us causes us to reflect *Jesus*, and allows us to attract others to *Him*. This is giving glory to God. As the Holy Spirit begins to produce His fruit in us, God, our Gardener, goes to work pruning us. The more we allow the Holy Spirit to control us, rather than our sinful flesh, the more of our sinful flesh God prunes away. The more that our sinful flesh is pruned away, the more abundant the fruit of the Spirit is in us. Let us allow the Holy Spirit full control of our lives so that they will be as fruitful as God has purposed them to be.

John 15:1–5, 8 (NLT); 2 Timothy 1:14 (NLT)

Day Eighty-Seven

You didn't choose me, remember; I chose you, and put you in the world to bear fruit, fruit that won't spoil. As fruit bearers, whatever you ask the Father in relation to me, he gives you. But remember the root command: Love one another.

John 15:16–17 (MSG)

We have learned much about fruit-bearing, and in the verse above, we see that Jesus tells us that we were put on this earth to bear fruit. In addition, the verse above tells us the "root command," which is to "love one another." This means that everything that we say and do must be done in love. First Corinthians tells us that if we didn't love others, we would be of no value whatsoever (1 Corinthians 13:3).

As we have seen in our look at the fruit of the Spirit, on our own and in our flesh, we may be capable of displaying many of the qualities of the fruit of the Spirit. There is a noticeable difference, however, between displaying these qualities from our flesh and displaying these qualities as a result of living by the Spirit. How are we to know the difference? How are we to know if we are being motivated by our flesh or by the Holy Spirit?

To answer those questions, we must look at what role love is playing. Are we exhibiting patience or kindness, or any of those qualities, in order to draw attention to ourselves, or perhaps, in an effort to seek God's approval? Or, are we exhibiting those qualities out of a genuine love for others? Do we truly desire to reflect Jesus to others, and help draw them to Him? We can be sure that we are following the Holy Spirit's lead if our motivation is love. Without the underlying motive of love, our efforts at displaying such qualities as patience, kindness, goodness, and gentleness are of no value whatsoever. The purpose of bearing fruit is to reflect Jesus and draw others to Him, accomplished when love is at the root.

1 Corinthians 13:1–7, 11–13 (NLT)

Day Eighty-Eight

As we know Jesus better, his divine power gives us everything we need for living a godly life. He has called us to receive his own glory and goodness! And by that same mighty power, he has given us all of his rich and wonderful promises. He has promised that you will escape the decadence all around you caused by evil desires and that you will share in his divine nature. So make every effort to apply the benefits of these promises to your life. Then your faith will produce a life of moral excellence. A life of moral excellence leads to knowing God better.

2 Peter 1:3–5 (NLT)

These verses are God's assurance to us that, as we strive to live our lives loving and following after Jesus, He will supply us with all that we need for living a godly life. God calls us to be blameless and pure, and to be holy in all we do, and He provides us with His Holy Spirit to enable us to live such godly lives. Before we knew Jesus, we didn't know any better; but, now that we know God's truth, God's Word, and God's will, we *do* know better. Because we know better, we are commanded not to live in our former ignorance. We are now to live changed lives.

As people who love and follow after Jesus, we are to look at Him as our Example. We are to take guidance and instruction from His Holy Word. The world around us cannot instruct us in living godly lives, so we cannot, and should not, follow after the ways of the world. God's Word calls the world we live in a dark world "full of crooked and perverse people" (Philippians 2:15, NLT). Does that mean that we should hole up and isolate ourselves from such a world? On the contrary, God tells us that we are to let our lives "shine brightly before them," (Philippians 2:15, NLT). As Christians, God commands us to live godly lives — to live in faithful obedience to Him and His Word. Our faithful, obedient living is designed to serve as a shining example to the world around us so that they may be saved.

Philippians 2:15 (NIV, NLT); 1 Peter 1:14–16;

1 Corinthians 10:33

Day Eighty-Nine

But we have this treasure in jars of clay to show that this all-surpassing power is from God and not from us.

2 Corinthians 4:7

For thousands of years, it has been customary to hide valuables or treasures in plain, ordinary containers so as not to draw attention to them. In biblical times, those treasures were typically concealed in clay jars. The message conveyed in the above verse is that the gospel, or the good news that Jesus is our Savior, is hidden within the hearts of all who believe. God has designed that Christian believers have this beautiful, treasured good news hidden inside of their ordinary, frail human bodies in order to showcase His magnificent power.

When we take that first step by believing that Jesus died and rose again for our sins, God makes "his light shine in our hearts to give us the light of the knowledge of the glory of God in the face of Christ"(2 Corinthians 4:6). As we believe in Him, Jesus makes His light, His home, in our hearts. When we choose to live in obedience to Him and the counsel He gives us through His Holy Spirit, God's *all-surpassing power* is unleashed in our lives. As we follow His lead, the Holy Spirit enables us to live godly lives, to bear the fruit of the Spirit, and to continually grow in our knowledge of Him.

As God's *all-surpassing power* goes to work in our lives

others take notice. As they see ordinary, frail people living godly lives and displaying godly characteristics, they glimpse a reflection of Jesus Himself. Their eyes are opened to see that it is not those ordinary, frail people who are the treasure, but the power of the treasure—Jesus—working *through* them. This knowledge attracts them to Jesus—the glorious treasure—who longs to do the same through them!

2 Corinthians 4:6; Galatians 4:6 (NCV); Philippians 4:13 (NLT)

Day Ninety

Teach me to do your will, for you are my God; may your good Spirit lead me on level ground.

Psalm 143:10

Here we are on the last day of our journey. Throughout these last ninety days, we have learned that Jesus longs for a personal relationship with us. We have learned that God calls us to continually bear fruit in our lives and to continually grow in our knowledge of Him. We have learned that God's ultimate goal for us is that we become more like Jesus. As His children, God has given us many and varied gifts, talents, abilities, and wisdom, but all with the purpose of reflecting Jesus and leading others to Him. That is God's will for us, and our purpose on this earth. Thankfully, God has given us His Holy Spirit to lead us and to keep us on the solid, "level ground" of a path walked with Him.

We are living in hard and troubling times. We live in a world that continually tempts us to put ourselves and our interests first and foremost, and to do whatever it takes to make sure we come out on top. We are surrounded by people who are godless and attempt to pull us away from our faith in God. Following God on the path He has marked out and chosen for us will not be easy or trouble free. But, as we keep persevering through this life, keeping our eyes on Jesus and living in obedience to the Holy Spirit's counsel, God will keep us sure and steady on the "level ground" of *His* Path. And, one day, He will take us to our eternal home, where He will say to us, "Well done, good and faithful servant! You have been faithful with a few things; I will put you in charge of many things. Come and share your master's happiness!"(Matthew 25:21).

Isaiah 30:21; Jeremiah 6:16a

Epilogue

Thank you for choosing to read this book. It is very personal to me, and my desire for you is that you discover, as I have, how rich and rewarding it is to walk the path of life with God. This is my prayer for you, from Colossians 1:9–14:

I pray that God will "fill you with the knowledge of his will through all spiritual wisdom and understanding." I pray "this in order that you may live a life worthy of the Lord and may please him in every way: bearing fruit in every good work, growing in the knowledge of God, being strengthened with all power according to his glorious might so that you may have great endurance and patience, and joyfully giving thanks to the Father, who has qualified you to share in the inheritance of the saints in the kingdom of light. For he has rescued us from the dominion of darkness and brought us into the kingdom of the Son he loves, in whom we have redemption, the forgiveness of sins."

Made in the USA
Lexington, KY
22 February 2015